Excel

Basic Skills

Comprehension and Written Expression

Year 6

Ages 11-12

Get the Results You Want!

PASCAL PRESS

Alan Horsfield

Reprinted 1999, 2001, 2002, 2004, 2005, 2006, 2008 (twice), 2009, 2011, 2012, 2013, 2014, 2018, 2020, 2022

ISBN 978 1 86441 281 9

Pascal Press
PO Box 250
Glebe NSW 2037
(02) 8585 4050
www.pascalpress.com.au

Published: Vivienne Joannou
Text design and typesetting by Scriptorium Desktop Publishing Pty Ltd
Cover by Dizign Pty Ltd
Printed by Vivar Printing/Green Giant Press

Contents

To the parent and teacher .... **iv**
Finding facts 1
Finding the main idea 7
Making inferences 13
Using context clues 17
Drawing conclusions 21
Noting detail 25
Following directions 29
Understanding questions 33
Understanding paragraphs 37
Relevant and irrelevant information 39
Fact and opinion 43
Understanding persuasion 47
Understanding and using a table of contents 51
Understanding and using an index 53
Using timetables 55
Understanding maps 57
Understanding graphs and charts 59
Answers (lift-out section) A1–A8

Acknowledgements

Elaine Horsfield of EJH Talent Promotion P/L for support, typing and proofreading, Cook Islands Library and Museum, Ian Rohr of Pascal Press who was always approachable; and those students who gave up their free time to 'test' the test writer.
CARROT CAKE White Wings Limited, The Crescent, Kingsgrove, NSW 2208 (from *Exploring procedure about cooking*, HBJ, 1990)
The Big Race by Alan Horsfield, Buzzwords, International Thomas Publishing, Australia, 1997
The Lemming Run by Alan Horsfield from *Then & Now*, Wannabee Publishing, 1997

To the parent and teacher

When students complete the exercises in this book they will have worked through a number of question types from a variety of types of texts.

Rather than give a range of question types based on each passage, the focus in this book will be on developing students' skill with a particular question type. The book is structured so that if there is a weakness or a 'gap' then students can concentrate on that particular weakness or 'gap' and become competent without working through passages that may not contribute to their progress.

With the help of an adult students will be able to focus on those skills that are appropriate.

Each new section provides information on what is required for the particular skill being practised. The first extract in each section is intended to lead students through a number of questions based upon a specific skill. Brief answers and guides for finding answers are provided at the end of the exercise. A full set of answers is provided in the middle of the book.

This book uses a range of types of texts so that students will feel confident in a variety of situations. Types of texts are usually broken into two broad categories which are literary and factual texts. Within each group are numerous varieties — some are listed below. All texts, except for the two timetables, the mobile phone ad and one small extract, are taken from the Pascal Press Spectrum Violet series or the associated teachers' resource books. The title of each book used is given at the start of each section. This allows the student to follow up exercises with recreational reading or reading for a specific purpose.

Literary texts include narratives (novels/stories), poetry and (drama) scripts.

Factual texts include explanations, expositions, information reports, recounts and procedures.

As you can see the list is quite long. It is important that students develop comprehension skills from a variety of types of texts. Many types of writing overlap.

On a number of occasions extracts are reused. This is done to demonstrate that different comprehension skills can be developed from the same piece of writing. Comprehension skills are interdependent.

As students' ability to comprehend increases they will also be expected to interpret data. This includes the interpretation of information in charts, tables and maps.

Question types include those that require:

- true or false responses
- multiple-choice responses
- short-answer responses
- full-sentence answers
- matching exercises
- sentence completion
- sequencing
- open-ended responses.

It is suggested that students should give full sentence answers unless directed otherwise. Sufficient space is allowed for such answers.

Good luck!

Alan Horsfield

Finding Facts — Introduction

When finding facts you will often be asked questions beginning with Who, When, Where, What and How, and sometimes Why. You will be asked to search for answers to questions that help you understand the **time (when)** and **place (where)** of the action in the extract, as well as **who** or **what** is involved. **Which** may also be used. Sometimes you will be asked to give **names** or make **lists**. In the following extract the words in brackets will help you find the facts. Often important facts are introduced by bullet points (•).

You will be asked to search for answers to questions that help you understand either factual material or narratives (stories).

Most exercises in this part of the book are based upon factual writing. **Indonesia** by Lisa Hill is a good place to start looking for facts. You should answer with full sentence answers unless told to do otherwise. Full sentence answers help you to think through the answer you are going to give.

Now read the extract from **Indonesia** by Lisa Hill.

The loudest explosion ever heard — when Krakatoa blew up!

(Where) Indonesia straddles one of the most unstable parts of the earth. There are many active volcanoes and earthquakes are common, so it is an interesting area for scientists to study fossil and geological activity.

(When/who) Javanese and Sumatran children found it hard to concentrate on school work in the afternoon of 26 August, 1883. In the straits between Java and Sumatra, 160 kilometres away, the little volcanic island of Krakatoa had been rumbling away for months. Until now, no one had taken much notice because the volcano had rumbled and puffed before, but now the grumbling was interrupted by sharp sounds like thunderclaps that echoed all over the islands.

(What/who) Terrified by the loud bangs, children rushed home to safety, but the noise was everywhere. No one slept much that night.

(When) Just before seven o'clock the next morning, two immense explosions shook the ground beneath their feet. Doors blew open, and walls cracked. Whole buildings shook. There was an enormous volcanic eruption in which 35 000 people were killed.

(Where) Nearly 3000 kilometres away in Australia, people heard what sounded like gunfire. The noise also reached Madagascar on the other side of the Indian Ocean, nearly 5000 kilometres from Indonesia. It was the loudest sound ever heard by human ears.

(What) The island of Krakatoa had ceased to exist.

1. Where is Indonesia situated? Indonesia ______________________.

2. What terrified the children? ______________________

3. When did Krakatoa explode? ______________________

4. Why did Krakatoa cease to exist? ______________________

5. Select the correct fact to complete this sentence: After the two big explosions

☐ children hurried from school. ☐ the volcano rumbled. ☐ many people were killed.

Short Answers 1. is situated on an unstable part of the earth. 2. loud bangs, 3. (7 o'clock on) 27 August 1883, 4. It had exploded. 5. many people were killed.

Finding Facts — Antarctica

by John Collerson

Why would anyone want to go to Antarctica? Would you go to a place that is dark for half the year and almost entirely covered with ice and snow? Even the ocean is frozen solid in some places or covered with floating pack-ice. It can snow in summer and it is usually so cold in winter that you can't go outside unless you are completely covered in thick clothes. The winds can blow with hurricane force for days on end. There are no trees and hardly any other plants, no land animals and no humans living there permanently. Until last century no one had even set foot on the place.

Yet people do go to Antarctica and they have been going there for more than 100 years. Today there are over 3000 people there in summer and about 1000 in winter. Why did people go there in the first place?

There was a time when no-one was even sure that Antarctica existed. The ancient Greek scholar who named it certainly hadn't been there. He just thought there must be some place at the opposite end of the world to the Arctic. That's what Antarctic means: the opposite of Arctic. Yet there were a few people curious enough to try to find out exactly what was there.

Captain Cook was one of these. He sailed into Antarctic waters in 1773 but didn't go far enough to see the land. When he got to a certain point, he decided that if there was any land still further south it must be covered with ice and snow all year round, so he turned back. However, on this voyage he did sail right round the world on the Southern Ocean.

But other mariners did press on. These included explorers, sealers and people who went because of scientific curiosity. They were driven by some sense of adventure, by the challenge of an unknown part of the world and a desire to get to the very end of the earth.

1. When did people first start going to Antarctica? ____________________

____

2. Who gave Antarctica its name? ____________________

3. What did Captain Cook do in the Southern Ocean? ____________________

Answer **True** or **False** to the facts in questions 4 to 7.

4. In 1773 Captain Cook saw Antarctica. __________

5. There are no trees in Antarctica. __________

6. The sun never shines in Antarctica. __________

7. About 1000 people spend their winter in Antarctica. __________

8. The first people to visit Antarctica were: (circle one answer)

Greek scholars mariners skiers whalers

9. Tick the two facts that best describe the harshness of Antarctica.

- ☐ Blizzards may last for days.
- ☐ The sea can freeze over.
- ☐ Nights can be very long.
- ☐ No humans live there permanently.
- ☐ Snow often falls in summer.

Finding Facts — Spacescape

by Karl Kruszelnicki

Saturn

Saturn is the second of the four gas giants. It is about 120 000 km across. Saturn takes 29.46 years to go round the Sun and, like Jupiter, it spins very rapidly. A day on Saturn lasts for only 10 hours and 39 minutes. Saturn has a similar structure to the planet Jupiter. Saturn is made up of a solid core, surrounded by a shell of liquid hydrogen. Finally, there is a giant shell of atmosphere. This atmosphere is made up of hydrogen and helium gases, ammonia and small amounts of other gases. Like Jupiter, Saturn seems to be a bubbling cauldron of liquid gases.

Saturn is also similar to Jupiter because the planet gives off more heat than it receives from the Sun. In the same way that steam gives off heat as it turns from gas into liquid, so helium gives off heat. On Saturn, the heat comes from the condensing of helium as it sinks in the atmosphere. Heat is also given off as the core of Saturn contracts, or grows smaller. This heat is the power supply that causes the weather on Saturn, for example, the fierce winds which travel at up to 1700 km an hour near the planet's equator.

While Jupiter has the Great Red Spot, Saturn has the Small Red Spot, which is about 6000 km across. Saturn also has the Great White Spot. This cloud of ammonia crystals seems to appear every 30 years and last appeared on 24 September 1990. The Great White Spot always appears in the mid-summer of the northern hemisphere of Saturn. During its last appearance, the Great White Spot very rapidly grew to an oval big enough to swallow three Earths and then stayed the same size for about three weeks. Then Saturn's strong winds began to change the Great White Spot and it became even larger, growing a long tail as it began to stretch around the planet, reaching some 240 km above the cloud tops.

Choose the best answer to complete questions 1 and 2.

1. Saturn's weather is different from Earth's weather because on Saturn

- ☐ there are no seasons.
- ☐ there are no clouds.
- ☐ the weather hardly ever changes.
- ☐ the winds are very strong.

2. Saturn is similar to Jupiter because it

- ☐ takes 29.46 years to circle the sun.
- ☐ has a Great White Spot.
- ☐ gives off more heat than it receives from the sun.
- ☐ is three times larger than Earth.

3. Titles guide the reader to important facts. Another good title for this extract would be:

- ☐ Voyage to Saturn.
- ☐ Saturn's weather.
- ☐ Life on Saturn.
- ☐ A day on Saturn.

4. Saturn consists of great quantities of gas. ☐ True ☐ False

5. The Great White Spot is a permanent feature of Saturn. ☐ True ☐ False

6. The Red Spot on Saturn is larger than the Red Spot on Jupiter. ☐ True ☐ False

Finding Facts — Earth First

by David Bowden & Jenny Dibley

The 'green revolution'

There is a revolution taking place in the minds of consumers around the world. It is known as the 'green revolution' or the era of environmentally-friendly shopping.

In the past, many consumers have not given their shopping habits and choices much thought. The need to think about what happens to products when they have been used has not, until recently, been an issue of concern.

In the past few years, however, consumers have become much more conscious of their shopping habits. People are now discussing the environment in terms of how everyone has a role to play in reversing this damage. Every time we buy a product, we consume resources that in some way deplete the environment. This is why it is time to rethink our shopping habits and choices.

There are many points to consider when buying a product. The cost of a product is usually the most important consideration for consumers. Comfort, size, shape, how fashionable the product is, and how it compares with similar products in terms of quality, is also important.

The 'green consumer' will also consider how the use of the product being purchased will affect the environment. Today's consumers should ask themselves the following questions before selecting a product:

- Has an animal suffered or died to make this product?
- Has energy been wasted to make this product?
- Is this product over-packaged?
- Is this product made from recycled materials?
- Were harmful chemicals used to make this product?
- Can this product be reused or recycled after it is used?
- Is this product really necessary?
- Has the environment been damaged by the making of this product?

Choose the best answer to complete questions 1 and 2.

1. According to the extract the 'green revolution' is mainly concerned with

☐ the cost of goods in supermarkets.

☐ whether or not goods are made from recycled material.

☐ how the production of the product will affect the environment.

☐ the amount of unnecessary packaging on many items.

2. A 'green consumer' is one who

☐ will not buy goods from a supermarket.

☐ considers many points before making a purchase.

☐ reuses all the packaging that comes with the purchase.

☐ will only damage the environment if the goods are not expensive.

3. The responsibility for a better environment lies with store owners. ☐ True ☐ False

4. For some shoppers, fashion is more important than the environment. ☐ True ☐ False

5. How many bullet points are used in this extract? ___________

6. Which bullet point would you consider most important when you go shopping? Why?

____

Finding Facts — Beowulf's Downfall

by Brad Turner

The story *Beowulf's Downfall* is an example of **realistic writing**. It is based upon **legend**, so it is a good book for 'finding facts' that are not from factual writing.

Wiglaf went immediately. The wealth he saw inside the mound thrilled him.

Gleaming gold lay everywhere. There were precious drinking cups, golden flagons, and cleverly-made ornaments. Best of all was the war flag that hung down from the ceiling. Made of the finest linen and embroidered with delicate gold wire, Wiglaf had never seen another to rival it.

Open mouthed, Wiglaf gazed for a moment longer. He then remembered his errand, and busied himself with gathering up only the very best treasures, including the war flag. Wiglaf worked quickly because he was afraid that Beowulf might die before seeing the wealth he had won from the dragon.

When he could carry no more, Wiglaf left the burial mound. Outside, he found Beowulf lying unconscious. The Gaut-king had fainted from loss of blood. Fearing the worst, Wiglaf dumped his load and snatched up his helmet. There was still some saltwater in it, which he sprinkled over Beowulf's face.

Slowly Beowulf came to his senses. He saw the treasures that Wiglaf had fetched and said: 'I give thanks to the Allfather for this treasure.'

Turning again to Wiglaf, Beowulf said: 'You must care for the people now. You are the last of the Waymundings, the only heir to the kingdom.'

King Beowulf then took off the heavy gold collar that he wore. It was the symbol of his right to rule Gautaland. Beowulf passed the collar to Wiglaf. He also gave the young earl his gold-plated helmet, his armour and his arm-ring. 'Use them all well,' he whispered. 'My time is done. Fate has lured each member of our family to their dooms. It was their courage that doomed them. Now I follow them.'

'Wiglaf, tell the warriors to build my burial mound upon Hronesness, where everyone can see it and remember me.' Those were Beowulf's last words …

1. Name the two characters in the extract. ______________ , ______________

2. Wiglaf entered the burial mound to

☐ kill the dragon.

☐ collect as much gold as possible.

☐ get help for Beowulf.

☐ get only those items of greatest value.

3. When Beowulf took off his golden collar and gave it to Wiglaf he was

☐ making him the new king.

☐ adding to their collection of gold.

☐ rewarding him for his work.

☐ trying to say his words clearly.

4. Circle the word that best describes Wiglaf's first feeling when he entered the mound.

fear greed worry pleased amazement

5. Beowulf wanted someone to rule over Hronesness after he died. ☐ True ☐ False

6. Beowulf had received his wounds in a battle with Wiglaf. ☐ True ☐ False

7. Wiglaf spent time carefully selecting the treasures for Beowulf. ☐ True ☐ False

Finding Facts — Eyes On The World

The Photojournalism of Bruce Miller

by David Bolliger

Imagine a world without photographs! I wonder if you can. And yet the camera was invented little more than 150 years ago. Back then photographs must have seemed like magic. People viewed them with a mixture of awe and suspicion.

Today photographs are a very ordinary part of our lives. Almost everybody in developed countries has a camera or at least access to one. Photographs are as common as words printed on a page.

In fact, photographs and the printed word have a lot in common. For a start, both words and photographs can tell stories and communicate information. And, with the help of sophisticated machinery, both words and photographs may be copied an unlimited number of times. The use of this machinery in the media means that within hours people all round the world can read the same story and look at the same pictures.

Do you remember learning to read? When you looked at a printed page you could see squiggles on paper, but you did not know what they meant. As surely as you needed to learn how these squiggles or symbols could mean something, you would need to learn how photographs can mean something.

This similarity between writing and photography is reflected in our use of language.

One important difference between writing and photography is that if you can't read, a page of printed or written words won't give you any message at all. But even if you have never learned to read photographs, you still get some message or take in some information when you look at them. This is because photographs look so much like a little piece of the world.

Once these have been copied on to photographic paper, the images have a life of their own. They are no longer the world you normally see; they are symbols of that world. Like words, these symbols can be used in many different ways to say many different things.

1. Draw a line from a sentence beginning to a sentence ending to make the facts correct.

If you can't read words	words seemed like squiggles on the paper.
Photographs look like	you can still get facts from pictures.
When you first started to read	a little piece of the world.

2. What is this extract about? The extract ____________________.

3. The first photographs were praised for their value. ☐ True ☐ False

4. Photographs can only be copied a limited number of times. ☐ True ☐ False

5. Machines can be used to copy words and photographs. ☐ True ☐ False

6. Write one fact you learnt from the extract. ____________________

____

7. Tick the best ending for this sentence. Photographs and words are similar because they

- ☐ were both invented about 150 years ago.
- ☐ need sophisticated machinery to produce them.
- ☐ are both used to tell stories.
- ☐ always mean exactly the same thing.

Finding the Main Idea — Introduction

When reading paragraphs you will often be asked to find the **main idea**. The main idea is often the same as the **topic sentence.** It is the most important piece of information for the reader. All other sentences in the paragraph add to the meaning of the topic sentence. They are often called the **supporting detail**.

The topic sentence is often the first sentence but it can come in the middle of the paragraph or at the end. The topic sentence, if it is quite long, may sometimes contain more information than just the main idea.

Paragraphs are usually made up of more than one sentence (see Understanding Paragraphs, p. 37). Titles and headings often give the main idea in books or in chapters. If we look at the extract, *Perfect Timing* by Jeremy Fisher we can use it to start 'finding the main idea'.

> This morning, the old house across the road seemed even lonelier than ever. **(main idea/ topic sentence)** Its empty windows, with only bare rooms behind them, looked like big, sad eyes, ready to weep. **(supporting detail)** It was the only house in the street that had a garden all the way around it, but this was summer dry: browned and wilted as there had been no-one to care for it. **(supporting detail)**
>
> Other houses were terraces or semi-detached, like Andrew's, and most had had new owners in the last few years. **(main idea/topic sentence)** They had been repainted, roofs had been fixed, and fences had been repaired or replaced. **(supporting detail)** But the big place opposite Andrew's house had been empty for eight months, since the old woman who lived there had died in her sleep, and it seemed to be slowly falling apart. **(supporting detail)** Andrew wondered if anyone would ever live there again. **(supporting detail)**
>
> It wasn't a long walk to school. **(main idea/topic sentence)** Except for Andrew, which was why he started earlier than his friends. As Andrew expected, Nick and Tim soon caught up with him. They were kicking a soccer ball back and forth as they strolled up the street. Nick had been given it for Christmas.
>
> Andrew was glad to see them, and being with them drove away the last of the sick feeling that starting school again had brought. **(main idea/topic sentence — single sentence paragraph)**

1. How many paragraphs are there in this extract from *Perfect Timing*? __________

2. How many topic sentences would you expect to find? __________

3. How many sentences of supporting details are there in the first paragraph? __________

4. Which of the following is the best heading for this extract? (circle one)

Playing soccer   Starting school   Repairing houses

5. Paragraph 2, is mainly about ______________________________ .

6. Paragraph 3 has support information about Andrew's walk to school. ☐ True ☐ False

7. The last paragraph has only one sentence. It is important because it explains (tick one box)

☐ why there is a big change in Andrew's mood. ☐ why Andrew was walking to school.

Answers 1. four, 2. four, 3. two, 4. Starting school (The other options are about details.), 5. houses in the street, 6. True, 7. why there is a big change in Andrew's mood.

Finding the Main Idea — Land of the Rippling Gold

by Una Clarke

Wendy blamed herself for the accident. If she hadn't been daydreaming out of the opposite window, she might have seen the stump and yelled in time for her father to turn the wheel. There wasn't another stump or tree on the roadside for miles. Besides, it was her fault they were even there, and now her mother sat covered with blood.

Two weeks had passed since her leg was gouged by Marjorie's bike. Christmas had come and gone. The slight wound had seemed to be healing, then suddenly swelled up in a shiny painful lump, putting her mother into a fine flap. Having suffered so dreadfully with a poisoned leg herself, and fearing for her child, she had insisted on consulting the doctor in the next town that very day. Her father, reluctant to lose a day's work, argued that a good poulticing would fix it. Edie had flared up at that, saying his family had said the same about her leg. So both parents had begun the journey in a grumpy mood.

They were barely out of town when it happened. Wendy remembered hearing her mother complain about losing a glove and her father's grunt as he bent down to pick it up, then the shock of the impact and his unaccustomed swearing as he jammed on the brake — too late!

1. The main event in the extract is about (tick one box)

- ☐ finding a lost glove.
- ☐ getting Wendy's leg treated.
- ☐ the passing of Christmas.
- ☐ how tree stumps can cause accidents.

2. Write the topic sentence for the first paragraph. ______________________________

____

3. Tick the box that is the main idea in the last paragraph. (tick one box)

- ☐ Wendy remembered hearing her mother complain.
- ☐ They were barely out of town when the accident happened.
- ☐ Her father grunted as he bent down to pick up the glove.
- ☐ Wendy's father jammed on the brakes.

4. Using your own words, how would you describe what is happening in paragraph 2?

____

5. Select the best title for this extract. (tick one box)

☐ Daydreams ☐ All in a day's work ☐ The accident ☐ Leg wound

6. Wendy blamed her father for the accident. ☐ True ☐ False

7. Wendy's mother was hurt in a motorbike accident. ☐ True ☐ False

8. The family was in the vehicle because of Wendy's accident. ☐ True ☐ False

Finding the Main Idea — Rainforests

by Stephen Jones

Rainforest structure

Despite the diversity of the species in them, tropical rainforests around the world share a number of common features.

The tropical rainforest is a layered environment. When we stand on the floor of a tropical rainforest we find it humid and dark. We also wonder where the bustling life that is supposed to be there is. In fact, most of it is above us in the **canopy**. Just beneath the canopy we have the hall of the forest which is made up of the trunks of trees and under our feet is the forest floor.

The canopy is the powerhouse of the tropical rainforest. It is often divided into three or more layers. Trees reach up, forming the canopy, capturing the Sun's rays that provide the energy for the whole ecosystem. So thickly do the leaves crowd that as little as one per cent of the light that falls on the canopy reaches the forest floor. Insects, spiders, centipedes, mammals, reptiles, amphibians and birds teem in the canopy 15 to 40 metres above the ground. Half of all the Earth's animals live in this environment.

While the top of the canopy is exposed to full sunlight and the wind, within and below the canopy it is darker, more humid and protected.

Towering above the canopy are the **emergents** — the tallest trees in the tropical rainforest. The environment around the crowns of these trees is quite different to that in the canopy. It is windier, less humid and sunnier. They do not host the masses of epiphytes that live in the canopy. Their seeds, like the feathery seeds of the giant kapok, are dispersed by the wind. Often they are the perches for eagles which hunt for food in the canopy.

It is not only the plant life that is layered. So too is the animal life. Many animals live in only one layer of the rainforest.

1. How many paragraphs in this extract? __________

2. What is the topic sentence for the third paragraph? ______________________________

____

3. The second last paragraph (starts with 'Towering . . . ') is about the very tops of trees.

Above the canopy conditions are (write one example) ______________________.

4. According to the extract, a rainforest is

- ☐ an environment of many levels.
- ☐ full of dangerous plants and animals.
- ☐ a bright, sunny place.
- ☐ 15m to 40m above the ground.

5. The word **emergents** refers to ______________ trees of the rainforest.

6. If you had to give the extract another title, a good one would be (tick one answer)

- ☐ The canopy.
- ☐ Life in the forest.
- ☐ Features of a rainforest.
- ☐ The world's tallest trees.

7. The opening paragraph introduces the reader to rainforests generally. ☐ True ☐ False

8. The third paragraph explains general differences in rainforest layers. ☐ True ☐ False

Finding the Main Idea — Dream Door of Shinar

by Patricia Bernard

As Kevin leapt through the doorway, he heard his father shout again but his angry voice was cut off as the Door slammed shut. He turned quickly, already regretting his impulsive action. What had made him do it? What had made him run through a doorway no one else could see?

The Door shimmered and became transparent. This time all he could see through it were trees. Tall trees with smooth, satiny trunks and long, thin leaves that hung like wisps of grey silk tied in bundles. Strange trees, his mind registered. Strange place!

He turned around. There were trees everywhere, lofty and towering, blocking out the light. Short, spindly saplings with silvery trunks clustered together, like a fence hemming him in.

So . . . his backyard had turned into a forest. A silent forest that made him feel as small as any of his ants. Some door!

He swung back to look at the Door but found only the ground littered with leaves. 'If I will it, maybe it'll appear again,' he said to himself, not very hopefully. Doors that came and went of their own accord probably couldn't be willed to appear just when he wanted them to.

Then he saw the ladder.

1. Which paragraph tells the reader that the door had disappeared? Paragraph _____

2. Draw a line to match the main idea in the paragraph with the paragraph number.

Paragraph 1	changed backyard
Paragraph 2	leaping through the Door
Paragraph 3	the Door begins to disappear

3. If you had to give the extract another title, a good title would be

- ☐ Giant ants.
- ☐ The strange Door.
- ☐ Leaves on the ground.
- ☐ Lost in the backyard.

4. Which paragraph suggests to the reader that Kevin may have changed size?

☐ Paragraph 4 ☐ Paragraph 5 ☐ Paragraph 6

5. Which event did NOT happen in the extract?

(A) Kevin's father followed him through the Door.

(B) The backyard was full of tall trees.

(C) The Door disappeared after a short time.

(D) Kevin was the only person who saw the Door.

6. The last paragraph is short because it tells of an important event. ☐ True ☐ False

7. It is most likely Kevin had been through the Door more than once. ☐ True ☐ False

8. Kevin was (angry concerned glad) that the Door had disappeared. (circle one word)

Finding the Main Idea — Perfect Timing

by Jeremy Fisher

Inside the hall, streamers and balloons were in profusion. Andrew recognised the streamers and decorations he had made among the many hanging from the ceiling and walls. He was pleased that the junk material they had gathered up and recycled had turned out looking so sharp.

Gaggles of kids stood about, talking excitedly about their clothes, their hair — for some of the boys had gone for a greased-back look, and several of the girls had teased their hair into towering beehives — and, of course, the band. At the end of the hall, on a small raised platform, stood a familiar drum kit. Guitars rested on their metal stands in front of it, and a keyboard system was arranged to one side. Large speakers had been placed on either side of the platform.

Nick and Tim ran up to Andrew and Amanda.

'Andrew,' Nick excitedly said, 'it's fantastic! They're really here. Even after winning the awards. They've still come to play for us!'

Right then, the lights dimmed. A hush fell over the hall, and all eyes fixed on the stage.

Suddenly lights flashed and — zap! — there was the band! They began their first song to the accompaniment of great multicoloured bursts of light which swirled about them.

Once they had finished, they began another of their hits, and then another. Andrew stood transfixed as the music rolled around him. It was as if he were suspended in space somewhere, seeing and hearing everything, but invisible to all about him.

Then the band finished their set. The applause went on and on. Nick and Matt were whistling and stamping their feet, and shouting out their approval. Andrew, out of his spell, had yelled himself hoarse. Amanda's hands were stinging from the number of times she'd clapped them together.

1. How many paragraphs in this extract? __________

2. What is the main idea (topic sentence) in the eighth paragraph? (tick one box)

- ☐ Then the band finished their set.
- ☐ The applause went on and on.
- ☐ Nick and Matt were whistling and stamping their feet, and shouting approval.
- ☐ Andrew, out of his spell, had yelled himself hoarse.
- ☐ Amanda's hands were stinging from the number of times she'd clapped them.

3. If you had to give the extract a title, a good title would be

- ☐ The award winning band.
- ☐ The big hit.
- ☐ Flashing lights.
- ☐ Whistling and stamping.

4. Nick was surprised the band had turned up to play. ☐ True ☐ False

5. The band played two songs before having a break. ☐ True ☐ False

6. The extract is mainly about the excitement of a concert. ☐ True ☐ False

7. When Nick arrived the band was already on the platform. ☐ True ☐ False

8. The crowd was (thrilled charmed amused) by the band. (circle one word)

Finding the Main Idea — Spacescape

by Karl Kruszelnicki

Saturn

Saturn is the second of the four gas giants. It is about 120 000 km across. Saturn takes 29.46 years to go round the Sun and, like Jupiter, it spins very rapidly. A day on Saturn lasts for only 10 hours and 39 minutes.

Saturn has a similar structure to the planet Jupiter. Saturn is made up of a solid core, surrounded by a shell of liquid hydrogen. Finally, there is a giant shell of atmosphere. This atmosphere is made up of hydrogen and helium gases, ammonia and small amounts of other gases. Like Jupiter, Saturn seems to be a bubbling cauldron of liquid gases.

Saturn is also similar to Jupiter because the planet gives off more heat than it receives from the Sun. In the same way that steam gives off heat as it turns from gas into liquid, so helium gives off heat. On Saturn, the heat comes from the condensing of helium as it sinks in the atmosphere. Heat is also given off as the core of Saturn contracts, or grows smaller. This heat is the power supply that causes the weather on Saturn, for example, the fierce winds which travel at up to 1700 km an hour near the planet's equator.

While Jupiter has the Great Red Spot, Saturn has the Small Red Spot, which is about 6000 km across. Saturn also has the Great White Spot. This cloud of ammonia crystals seems to appear every 30 years and last appeared on 24 September 1990. The Great White Spot always appears in the mid-summer of the northern hemisphere of Saturn. During its last appearance, the Great White Spot very rapidly grew to an oval big enough to swallow three Earths and then stayed the same size for about three weeks. Then Saturn's strong winds began to change the Great White Spot and it became even larger, growing a long tail as it began to stretch around the planet, reaching some 240 km above the cloud tops.

1. Using your own words, write what paragraph 1 is about. (main idea) ____________________

____

2. The second paragraph is mainly about the (tick one box)

☐ structure of Saturn. ☐ position of Saturn.

☐ age of Saturn. ☐ life on Saturn.

3. The last paragraph is mainly about the

☐ Great White Spot of Saturn. ☐ wind speeds on Saturn.

☐ atmosphere (air) on Saturn. ☐ best times to view Saturn.

4. Saturn's core is made up of bubbling gases (paragraph 2). ☐ True ☐ False

5. A day on Jupiter lasts a little more than 10 hours. ☐ True ☐ False

6. Saturn and Jupiter are similar planets in a number of ways. ☐ True ☐ False

7. Write the topic sentence for the last paragraph. (be careful) ____________________

____

8. Information about Jupiter's rapid spinning is in the first paragraph. This information is (tick one box) ☐ supporting detail. ☐ the main idea.

Making Inferences — Introduction

Making an inference is a thinking or reasoning skill (see also Drawing Conclusions p. 21). The reader is often only given a limited amount of information. The reader makes inferences from the information given. Readers also use their general knowledge when making inferences.

Read the following short passage.

> Claude McGhee was in Year Six. He was the biggest kid in school, and he hadn't got his nickname, Claws, for nothing. He was built like a bear but he could also run.
>
> from *The Big Race*, A. Horsfield

The reader could make several inferences from this passage. What sort of a person is Claude McGhee? How did he *really* get his nickname? From the evidence, the reader could probably **infer** that Claws was a bully, or someone to be frightened of. The reader could also make some **inferences** about the narrator and how he feels.

Sometimes writers will deliberately mislead the reader. They do not give all the information or they add information that gives the reader the wrong ideas or impressions. This happens in mystery stories and some scary (horror) books.

Now read the extract from *The Crystal Key* by Pamela O'Connor.

> Emma's heart was in her mouth as they entered the third underground level. It smelled dank and dirty, not at all like the pleasant earthy smell of the two higher levels.
>
> 'It even *smells* evil,' she whispered as they crept in single file along a dark tunnel.
>
> 'Yes,' Joel whispered back. 'There are bad vibrations down here. We must be very careful not to think about failure. Our thoughts must remain positive.'
>
> They stumbled through the darkness towards a faint pinpoint of light. They stopped for a moment while Joel went a little way ahead, trying to get his bearings. In the deep gloom Emma and Chris saw him beckon them forward.
>
> They were just about to move off again when Emma heard a sudden gasp behind her. She swung around.
>
> 'Chris!' she whispered hoarsely. There was no answer, and she could see no sign of her brother. 'Chris!'
>
> She felt panic rising and began to run back along the tunnel when a hand reached out and grabbed her tightly around the wrist. 'Sshh!' Joel's voice hissed close to her ear. 'Don't move!'

1. The reader could infer that the children are in a risky situation. What information makes the reader think this? ______________________________

2. What information has Pamela O'Connor given to imply that Joel is a sensible person?

____

3. What happens that helps to create a scary feeling? ________________________

4. The tunnel is scary. This can be inferred from the fact that (tick one box)

☐ it is deep and dark. ☐ there is a pinpoint of light. ☐ Emma was grabbed.

Short answers 1. Several answers: Chris doesn't answer; Emma's heart was in her mouth; The tunnel 'smells' evil, 2. Joel remains calm 3. Possible answers: Chris gasps/Chris doesn't answer/ Joel hisses 'Don't move!' 4. it is deep and dark.

Making Inferences — Dream Door Of Shinar

by Patricia Bernard

The Nest

With infinite care, the Queen's sensitive antennae inspected the bread. Suddenly she reared up on her back legs, flung the loaf to the ground, and with a scream that pierced Cloud's brain, launched herself at the girl.

As her hairy front legs hit Cloud's shoulders and her middle legs grabbed her waist, the alerted sentry ants dropped the bread and swarmed over the two bodies, adding their weight to that of the Queen's egg-filled stomach. Cloud was dragged to the floor.

Kevin swung his torch at an attacking ant.

Thurt, a flaming torch in one hand, the long handled axe in the other, swung at the group of three.

The rest of the ants swarmed over Cloud and their Queen.

'Fight them!' tapped out the Queen.

The sentry ants let go of Cloud and turned on Thurt and Kevin, as did Cloud, who grabbed for Kevin's torch, and would have burned her hands if he hadn't snatched it back.

'Look out for the Queen', warned Kevin. 'She's curling her tail ready to sting.'

Thurt swung his axe as hard as he could. Connecting with the two sentry ants and the Queen ant's thorax, he knocked the three of them into the air.

The Queen screamed furiously as she hit the ground. With her sting curled into position she charged spindle-legged at Thurt.

1. The reader can infer that the ants are as big as the children. How is this suggested?

____

2. The children had planned to be in the nest. Which statement supports this inference?

☐ The sentry ants were ready to attack. ☐ The boys carried flaming torches.

☐ The Queen ant was ready to sting. ☐ Cloud was knocked to the ground.

3. Who was closest to the Queen before the attack? (Tick one box)

☐ Kevin ☐ Cloud ☐ Thurt

4. Give a reason for your answer to Q. 3. (full sentence) ______________________________

____

5. Who was the most daring of the children? (Tick one box)

☐ Kevin ☐ Cloud ☐ Thurt

6. Give a reason for your answer to Q. 5. (full sentence) ______________________________

____

7. The Queen ant suspects there is something wrong with the bread. ☐ True ☐ False

Making Inferences — Through the web and other stories

Note: Sometimes a story is written by one of the characters. We call that person the narrator.

Through the web

by Ellen Robertson

My mother tells me I can't live in darkness forever. I keep the curtains drawn so that the mess doesn't look quite so bad. Imagine how I felt when I finally had to open the curtains, and found a massive spider's web spun into one of the corners of the window, directly above my head.

Night after night I have been sleeping just centimetres away from certain death. Do you think my mother knew about it? If she did, why didn't she do something about it?

I reacted very calmly: 'Hey Mum, there's a ginormous spider's web in here!' I screamed.

She was equally calm. 'Get the broom and sweep it away Lyndell.'

Just like that. Sweep it away, she says. I examined it closely — well, as closely as The Guide to Poisonous Spiders and I determined to be safe. The strange thing was that although the web was huge, I couldn't see a spider.

Now by my reckoning, that spider would have to be about as big as my fist. I tried telling this to my mother. She told me to stop exaggerating. One of the unfortunate things about being a teenager is that adults rarely believe you.

1. Who is the narrator of this extract? ______________________

2. From the extract you can infer that Lyndell (tick as many boxes as you need)

☐ reacts without getting all the facts. ☐ has to live in a room with no light.

☐ doesn't expect her mother to do everything. ☐ has a vivid imagination.

3. From information in the extract, Lyndell's mother could be best described as (tick one box)

☐ demanding. ☐ practical. ☐ hard working. ☐ stressed.

4. Lyndell keeps the curtain closed to keep out spiders. ☐ True ☐ False

5. The sight of the spider really frightened Lyndell. ☐ True ☐ False

6. Why do you think Lyndell was reading *The Guide to Poisonous Spiders*? (Give your reason.) ______________________

7. It can be inferred that Lyndell's mother's reaction to Lyndell is a result of

(A) Lyndell being a teenager.

(B) Lyndell's habit of exaggerating.

(C) Lyndell having a messy room.

(D) Lyndell's screams.

Making Inferences — Night of the Muttonbirds

by Mary Small

The storm lasted three days. Harsh icy winds blew keenly in from the south. People kept to their houses, warming themselves by wood stoves and fires, while the islands, smothered by clouds and battered by angry seas, waited for the storm to pass.

As evening approached on the third day there was a sudden **lull** in the wind and the grey clouds dispersed, revealing a pale watery sun over the western horizon. A broad belt of glistening white light spread across the swollen sea and one by one each rain-blurred, wave-beaten island stood out in sharp relief.

As the sun dipped, there appeared on the eastern horizon a cloud, darker and more definite than the wind-torn fragments still lacing the evening sky. It moved close to the face of the sea; a strange rising then falling undulation that grew increasingly larger and denser as it came closer. Within this cloud flew **millions** of shearwaters skimming the surface of the waves, making full use of the up-draughts and currents to bank then glide on their sickle-shaped wings. They flew with an urgency; an urgency that had propelled them from half a world away over limitless horizons towards these Bass Strait islands, their summer breeding grounds. Many were exhausted, and some had been lost on the way through battling strong headwinds.

Night came early as the bird cloud curtained the rising moon and converged landward. Over granite outcrops and sandhills, dark forms flitted and swept low as each bird circled then recircled to locate its burrow from the previous year, the only sound being the whispering swishing of wings stroking the air. Gradually, the dark cloud disintegrated as one by one small shadows folded their wings and **dropped**, plummeting awkwardly into the thick spiny tussock grass.

1. From the extract you can infer that the birds (shearwaters) **dropped** to the island because they had (tick one box)

   ☐ been hurt. ☐ become exhausted from flying.

   ☐ been caught in a storm. ☐ found their nesting place.

2. Sometime we can infer the meaning of a word from the words around it (its context). What word do you think could best replace 'lull'?

   ☐ calm ☐ chill ☐ increase ☐ fury

3. It is implied that the people of the island lived very simple lives. Which statement supports this inference? (tick one box)

   ☐ The people keep out of the wind. ☐ The houses are kept warm with wood fires.

   ☐ The island has a very harsh climate. ☐ The grass on the island is spiny tussock grass.

4. The birds waited for the storm to pass before coming to the island. ☐ True ☐ False

5. The swarm of birds appeared just before sunset. ☐ True ☐ False

6. What words other than 'million' informs the reader that there were many birds?

   ☐ They flew with an urgency ☐ dark forms flitted and swept low

   ☐ curtained the rising moon ☐ rain-blurred, wave-beaten island

Using Context Clues — Introduction

Sometimes, when we read, we are not always directly told all the information. Often we can work out what is happening, how people feel or where the action is by information in the writing. The context can also give clues to the meaning of new or unusual words.

Read this short passage.

But it was the bodies — packed together on the street — waiting. The crowd wasn't unruly. It was quiet, subdued, fending off the winter chill by sheer bulk of numbers. Like penguins guarding their eggs during a winter blizzard. Forever slowly swirling, never wanting to be exposed to the elements, to the dangers of being left exposed and vulnerable on the outer ring of the masses. Men and women, but mostly men, talking to one another in secretive tones.

The Lemming Run, A. Horsfield

From the text we get clues about what might be going on: something sinister seems about to happen (many people waiting in the cold). They seem frightened (no one wants to be on the edge of the crowd). We get this information from the **context** in which it appears. We use context clues.

Read this extract from *The Crystal Key* by Pamela O'Connor.

'I don't see why I should have to clean up after him!' Emma yelled rudely at her mother. 'It's his mess just as much as mine! Tell him to pick it up.'

Mrs Kelly sighed. She really couldn't be bothered arguing with her daughter over who had messed up the living room. As her mother picked up the articles of clothing, books and games that were lying around, Emma stormed out of the room.

'I just don't know what's come over that child lately,' Mrs Kelly grumbled to the vacuum cleaner. 'I can't ask her to do anything without her behaving as if she's being treated like a slave or something.' The vacuum whirred noisily as Mrs Kelly continued her solitary conversation. 'It seems to me I'm the only slave around here!'

Meanwhile, Emma was making her way down to her Auntie Tahlia's bookshop.

Tahlia wasn't really Emma's aunt. She and Mrs Kelly had been friends since they were in kindergarten together. Emma often thought it was an unlikely friendship. Her mother was so straight and old-fashioned. And while Emma thought she was pretty and always looked clean and fresh, she had no **style** and her clothes were totally boring.

1. We can tell the Kelly family are not really poor because (tick one box)

- ☐ Mrs Kelly has a friend.
- ☐ the children own many things.
- ☐ they have a slave to do the work.
- ☐ Mrs Kelly keeps her clothes clean.

2. How often, do you think, the mother and daughter argued? (give your reason) ________

____

3. The word **style** in this extract means (fashion sense   uniform). (circle one answer)

4. Emma could best be described as thoughtful and considerate. ☐ True ☐ False

Short answers 1. the children owned many things. 2. Often, because Mrs Kelly can't ask Emma to do anything without Emma getting upset. 3. fashion sense, 4. False

Using Context Clues — Courageous Crew

by Kathleen Allanby

The clucky hen, that Mr Mick had given to Victoria and the boys (Hyam and Ned), had hatched out chickens which they kept for a time in a wire-netting coop in the barn. But now Brindy could look after her family well enough herself, although once her distressed squawking made them all rush outside.

Slender and light on her feet, Victoria was first up the steps of the bank. Brindy was flapping and squawking in alarm, and hustling her chickens towards the open end of the barn.

What was wrong? Victoria looked all around, shading her eyes from the sun. There was nothing that she could see. Then above the sound of the bush sighing in the breeze she heard the swish-swishing of wings and looked up. An eaglehawk was swooping towards her out of the sky. Squealing, she dropped into a crouch, flinging her arms round her head.

The boys rushed up, shouting and waving their arms at the eaglehawk. It soared round and swept away to look for easier prey in the hills.

'It was after the chickens, nitwit, not you,' grinned Hyam as Victoria stood up. 'Cor, knew you were scared of spiders, but a bird — fair dinkum!'

From then on Brindy seemed to think she owned the barn. She was in there when Hyam and Ned went in to peg out their skins. She scurried outside with her chickens, clucking indignantly, and a cackling fowl flew off the nest somewhere around the loose hay. They stretched the rabbit skins over wire frames and hung them on nails in the wall and tacked out the possum skins flat against the outside wall to dry. Then, going back into the barn, they searched for the nest of the cackling fowl.

1. Give two examples that suggest to the reader that Hyam and Ned were well organised.

a) ______________________ **b)** ______________________

2. It is most likely the eagle was swooping down because it

- [ ] was about to attack Victoria.
- [ ] had been frightened by the screaming.
- [ ] had seen the hen with the chickens.
- [ ] was about to snatch an animal skin.

3. On what kind of a day do you think the eagle appeared? (Give your reasons) __________

____

4. Hyam thought that Victoria's reactions to the eagle had shown that she was

(brave careless useful timid considerate). (circle one word)

5. From information in the extract it is most likely that Brindy is a

- [ ] close friend of Victoria's.
- [ ] worker who helps on the farm.
- [ ] person who lives in the barn.
- [ ] hen with a brood of chickens.

6. The brooding hen in the barn had been disturbed by Victoria. ☐ True ☐ False

7. Rabbit skins and possum skins are dried using the same method. ☐ True ☐ False

Using Context Clues — Do They Play Marbles On Mars?

by Margaret McAlister

'I saw that, Michael!' said Mrs Jackson. 'Come out here!'

'What?' I tried to look innocent. 'What did I do?'

Mrs Jackson sighed. She looked up at the ceiling then back at me.
'Apologise to Cheryl.'

Now, that was *really* heavy. It was only a bit of screwed-up paper. Nobody ever died from being hit on the head by an old maths test.

Cheryl **smirked**. I glared at her. Cheryl had done much worse things to me. Mrs Jackson hardly *ever* caught *her*. I should have just dobbed Cheryl in for letting that matchbox full of ants loose in my lunch box.

'Go ahead, Michael,' said Mrs Jackson. 'Unless you'd like to pick up papers for a week.'

I thought about it for a moment. It would almost be worth it to choose the papers, but then I thought of Cheryl following me around all week yelling insults while I picked up the rubbish. Then I would be forced to stuff some dirty, sticky iceblock wrappers down her T-shirt . . . and then I would get two weeks of picking up papers . . .

'Sorry,' I muttered, looking at the floor.

1. Mrs Jackson is most likely (tick one box)

☐ Cheryl's mother. ☐ Michael's mother. ☐ a teacher. ☐ a cleaner.

2. Michael said he was sorry because

☐ Cheryl had been really hurt. ☐ it was better than picking up papers.

☐ he hadn't meant to be nasty. ☐ he had been in the wrong and knew it.

3. When Mrs Jackson looked up at the ceiling she was

☐ expecting something to fall from the ceiling.

☐ pretending to be bored by Michael's answer.

☐ wondering if she was about to get hit on the back of the head.

☐ having trouble with her eyes.

4. How well did Michael and Cheryl get on? Give your reasons. ____________________

____

5. Why did Michael look at the floor when he apologised? ____________________

____

6. The word 'smirk' means to smile (happily meanly sweetly). (circle one word)

7. Michael had been in a long-term 'fight' with Cheryl. ☐ True ☐ False

Using Context Clues — Courageous Crew

by Kathleen Allanby

After searching **every nook and cranny** at Woodlands for Denny's cat, the boys and Victoria set off through the bush to Kennelley's place. On the way they called in at the blacksmith's shop where Abe was clipping a horse.

'Seen a white cat?' asked Hyam.

Abe straightened up, shifting his weight onto one leg. 'A white cat, now ... can't say that I have, but I'll ask whoever comes along — **spread the word around**, so t'speak.'

A farmer was turning the handle of the clippers, and Abe worked on round the horse's flank, shaving up to a straight line along its belly. 'Shave him **clean as a whistle** underneath,' he said, 'so he won't get sore when he sweats.'

Leaving Abe, they went on up the hill and saw Mr Mick in the orchard. Denny darted ahead. 'Mr Mick!' Rushing up to him, he cried, 'Mr Mick, one of us is missing. Whitey hasn't come for her dinner.'

Mr Mick rested a hand on his back. 'I wouldn't worry too much, old fella. Plenty of tucker out in the bush. She'll turn up.'

But day followed day with Denny **mooching** around Woodlands listening for a sound on the wind.

1. Do you agree the incident in the extract most likely happened many years ago? Give your reason. ______________________

2. When someone says they will 'spread the word around' they mean they will

☐ let anyone they meet know what is happening. ☐ put up a large sign for all to see.

☐ check out the newspapers for details. ☐ make a note of the information.

3. Abe's reaction could be described as (considerate uncaring). (circle one word)

4. The word '**mooching**' suggests that Denny was

☐ bored. ☐ worried. ☐ tired. ☐ disinterested.

5. Mick rested his hand on his back. This suggests he was (old aching thinking). (circle one word)

6. Most people were not too worried about the lost cat. ☐ True ☐ False

7. To search '**every nook and cranny**' means to search everywhere. ☐ True ☐ False

8. Name two adults Denny spoke to about the lost cat.

a) ______________ b) ______________

9. When people say something is 'as clean as a whistle' they mean it is

☐ very clean. ☐ rough and prickly.

☐ only half washed. ☐ in need of a cleaning.

Drawing Conclusions — Introduction

Drawing conclusions is an advanced reading skill. It requires you to make a judgment about what you have read. It involves finding the **main idea** (p. 7), **making inferences** (p. 13) and using **context clues** (p. 17). It is related to other reading skills such as identifying **fact and opinion** (p. 43) and being able to distinguish between **relevant and irrelevant information** (p. 39).

A conclusion is reached by reasoning (thinking about a situation). It may be required that you have an opinion or make a decision. You may have to justify your opinion or reason. Drawing conclusions can only be done after you have read the whole extract (or story). Only then will you have all the information you need.

Read this extract from *The Miners Rest* by Robert L Muddyman.

George re-read the letter, hoping that he may have misunderstood its meaning. The first part was clearly a statement for the rates owing on the Miners Rest; however, it was the section entitled 'Remarks' that was the reason for his concern. He turned to Terrie who had just entered the room carrying some tins of paint. 'What do you make of this?'

Terrie sensed the concern in her husband's voice and stopped to listen.

George read out the section carefully; 'At a recent meeting of the Council, it was brought to our attention that some time has elapsed since you were issued with a permit to renovate the property known as the Miners Rest. As no request has been received by this department for inspection of work completed, a member has been instructed to call within the next few days. In the event that the work is not being carried out to Council satisfaction, an order of demolition will be issued. Signed, G. W. Featherby, Shire Engineer.'

Terrie took her husband's hand. 'It means exactly what it says, George,' she said calmly.

George shrugged his shoulders. 'That's it then, isn't it? We've had it! I thought we'd have a couple of years at least.'

Terrie searched for an answer. 'If we asked for an extension, surely . . . '

George shook his head. 'Three months at the most. Sorry, love, we just haven't got the sort of money that's needed to finish the place in time and if we don't call it quits soon, we're going to come out of this flat broke.'

1. Terrie has an optimistic (positive) attitude. Name two occasions when Terrie displays such an attitude. ______________________

____

2. What information leads you to the conclusion that for George and Terrie the Miners Rest is important to them? ______________________

3. George could be best described as (careful concerned curious). (circle one answer)

4. A good title for the extract would be (Shire Engineer Unexpected Letter). (circle one)

5. What information leads you to the conclusion that the Council is not being unfair?

____

Answers 1. She keeps calm. She suggests a solution to the problem. 2. They had spent some time (stated in Council letter) and money renovating the Miners Rest. 3. concerned, 4. Unexpected Letter, 5. The letter was friendly/formal. George and Terrie had had some time to complete the work. (see Council letter).

Drawing Conclusions — Do They Play Marbles On Mars?

by Margaret McAlister

We all piled outside to lunch. Everyone was talking about Mrs Beeste. She was terrible. She was a slave driver. She was a mean horrible bully ...

But I wondered about her.

She had made sure nobody nicked my marbles. That was good. But then, she didn't give them back.

She said we still had to do the play ... but that we might get 'a big surprise'.

Mrs Beeste was quite confusing.

Lunchtime was boring. Usually, I tried to eat lunch in about five minutes so I could play marbles. Today I had no marbles. And no-one would lend me any. They were happy I was out of the game for a while. I won too often.

I wandered over to the skipping.

Cheryl saw me. 'Wanna play?' she asked. Then she laughed at me. She didn't think I could skip. As if anyone couldn't do that. Hop. Hop. Hop. Cinchy. I decided to show her.

'Sure,' I said. 'Nothing else to do.'

I found I quite like skipping. Until Cheryl took the end of the rope. Then it was painful. Suddenly the rope developed a nasty habit of whipping my legs. Cheryl pulled it high and tight, so I'd trip.

'You're cheating,' I yelled.

'Am not,' she said, grinning and pulling the rope tighter.

1. Circle the letters that go with the sentences that let you draw the conclusion that the narrator was not aware of Cheryl's purpose. (You might have to read the extract again.)

(A) He had lost his marbles to Mrs Beeste.

(B) No one would lend him marbles.

(C) He joined in the skipping on Cheryl's first invitation.

(D) He was ready to jump rope when it became fast and tight.

2. What information leads you to the conclusion that Cheryl was being mean? (give one reason) ____________________

3. The narrator could best be described as seeing himself as (a 'big shot' misjudged). (circle your choice)

What information leads you make this conclusion? (tick two reasons)

- ☐ Mrs Beeste had taken his marbles.
- ☐ He didn't understand Mrs Beeste.
- ☐ He thought he was good at skipping.
- ☐ He was interested in the 'big surprise'.
- ☐ He let himself be taunted by Cheryl.
- ☐ Cheryl had not wanted him to join in.

4. Mrs Beeste was NOT well liked by the students. What information leads you to this conclusion? ____________________

5. You can conclude that girls and boys got on well together. ☐ True ☐ False

Drawing Conclusions — Australia's Unwritten History

by Oodgeroo Noonuccal

Legends are very special to all cultures.

Gwondo the Dolphin

Gwondo was the trainer of dogs. He would go out every day with his dogs, to teach them how to ambush the animals so all the tribe could eat. He had an elongated head, and his dark hair was interrupted by a crest of white hair that shone in the sunlight. It was just like the crest on the head of a cockatoo, only Gwondo's crest was white.

Wherever Gwondo went, his tribe could see him away in the distance on the hills, because his white hair would shine in the sunlight. The tribal elders would say to their children, 'See, there is Gwondo and his dogs, searching for food for us all.' Gwondo went hunting every day and he always came back to the camp with much food for his tribe. And all were very happy.

Now Gwondo grew old and as all mortals do, one day he died. The tribe mourned his loss, for he was much loved and the camp wailed many days and many nights.

Until one day the elders called to their children. 'You have wailed enough for Gwondo. Now it is time to start thinking about living. Go down to the beach and be happy.'

The children ran down to the beach and looked out to sea. Suddenly they all looked at each other, then turned and ran back to their elders, calling to them. 'Come quickly. Gwondo, he is back with us. He is out in the sea.'

The elders ran down to the beach and they nodded their heads and said, 'Yes it is Gwondo come back from his old Dreamtime to a new Dreamtime. He is now a dolphin and lives in the sea.'

Now whenever you see a school of dolphins in the sea, look for the big old dolphin. You will recognise him because he has a large white fin on his back. He is Gwondo and he is training the young dolphins to chase fish close to shore so that his tribe will be able to catch them.

Gwondo is known to all the tribes on the east coast of Australia. They call him their sea dog.

1. Circle the letters that go with the information that let you draw the conclusion that this is a legend. (You might have to read the extract again.)
   (A) Gwondo trains dolphins to chase fish close to the shore.
   (B) Dolphins are known to all tribes down the eastern coast.
   (C) Gwondo went out every day to get food for the tribe.
   (D) Gwondo had some white hair on his head.
   (E) Children, playing on the beach, recognised Gwondo.

2. What information leads you to the conclusion that there is a connection between dogs and dolphins? Both take part in ________________________ .

3. The elders (wanted didn't want) the children to play on the beach. (circle your choice)
What information helps you make this conclusion? (tick your reasons)
☐ The children had been mourning for too long.
☐ There were no fish to catch from the shore.
☐ They were afraid that Gwondo would return.

4. You can conclude that the elders didn't expect Gwondo to return. ☐ True ☐ False

Drawing Conclusions — Technology For The Environment

by Mike Callaghan & Peter Knapp

Soil erosion

Soil erosion is the natural process where soil is carried away by water and wind and deposited somewhere else, usually at the bottom of the ocean. Usually, the process of erosion is balanced by the processes which build the soil up. Scientists estimate that the natural process of soil formation can take from 100 to 2500 years to produce about 2.5cm of topsoil, which contains the nutrients necessary for plant growth.

Plants and trees hold the topsoil in place. When plants and trees are removed, the topsoil is exposed and is easily washed away by rain, or blown away by the wind. The wrong use of technology and poor land management can destroy soil that took millions of years to develop, in just ten years.

The natural process of erosion has increased since humans began to plough the soil for crops and clear the land to feed large numbers of grazing animals. Bad land management practices, such as ploughing and clearing steep slopes, using too much irrigation and having too many animals grazing on pastures, all help to remove vegetation and leave the soil open to the effects of wind and rain. Perhaps the most destructive practice is the removal of forest. At present, we remove 12 million hectares of forest each year. Because of all of these practices, the world loses approximately 75 billion tonnes of soil each year. At this rate, we will lose 18 per cent of the farmable land on earth by the year 2000.

Another problem is soil salinity. Soil salinity refers to the amount of salt in the soil. If soil has too much salt it will kill the plants already growing and will not allow new ones to grow. The total area of saline soil in Australia is 3.4 per cent. Scientists estimate that the large area of saline soil is the result of poor land management. There are two main causes of soil salinity: irrigation and dryland. Dryland happens when trees and other vegetation are removed from hilltops which results in more water soaking into the ground.

1. Soil erosion is considered a modern day problem. Tick the boxes that allow you to draw this conclusion. (You might have to read the extract again.)
   - ☐ People cause all soil erosion.
   - ☐ People plough the soil to grow crops.
   - ☐ There is more wind nowadays.
   - ☐ Eroded soil ends up in the ocean.
   - ☐ There is too much crop irrigation.
   - ☐ Forests are being removed on steep slopes.
2. What fact leads you to the conclusion that the removal of trees is a major cause of soil erosion. (give one reason) ____________________
3. Soil salinity is (natural   a result of poor farm management). (circle one answer)
4. The removal of trees is a major cause of salty soils. ☐ True ☐ False
5. To reduce the amount of soil erosion it is important that (tick all the boxes you need)
   - ☐ people grow more crops.
   - ☐ the rainfall be reduced.
   - ☐ more trees are planted.
   - ☐ less land is irrigated.
6. It would be safe to conclude that soil erosion is going to get worse. ☐ True ☐ False
7. Forests are being removed at the rate of 75 billion hectares a year. ☐ True ☐ False
8. The removal of trees on hillsides results in erosion and salinity. ☐ True ☐ False

Noting Detail — Introduction

Detail plays an important part in written works. Details help to give the reader a clear understanding of the story or the topic. Details can give different types of writing its particular 'flavour'. Details often allow the reader to draw conclusions (see p. 21).

When looking at detail we must determine whether or not it is appropriate (see **Relevant and irrelevant information** p. 39)

Look at this extract from *Forbidden Territory* by Kathleen Allanby.

> Neil came out of the anaesthetic in a long ward. Lights were on; he could hear faint stirrings and footsteps further away. An old man lay in the next bed crumpled under the bedclothes. Wriggling higher on the pillow Neil saw that Sister must have worked something out for across the aisle was the red haired man. In dressing gown and slippers he was sitting on the edge of his bed with his injured hand in a sling.

We read that Neil is in hospital. The detail gives the reader an idea of what it is like to wake up after anaesthetic.

1. How do the 'details' suggest that Neil is gradually becoming more aware? The details that tell us how Neil is slowly becoming aware of his situation: first the light, then sounds, then the person in the next bed and finally the old man across the aisle.

2. What 'detail' suggests that the red-haired man was not seriously hurt? ______________

____

3. What 'detail' suggests that Neil had spent some time in the hospital before he was put under anaesthetic? ____

Continue your reading of the extract from *Forbidden Territory*.

> 'You awake, eh?' He came towards Neil with a magazine. 'How's the leg? It'll slow you down for a bit.'
>
> 'No worries!' grinned Neil.
>
> 'Something to read.' He dropped down the magazine and pulled up a chair. 'I'm Dan O'Dowd, and you?'
>
> 'Me? I'm Neil . . . Neil Sparks. Is it okay to call you Uncle Dan? We call all House Parents 'Uncle' and 'Aunt'. There'll be another lot there at Christmas time — just them and me and Brown.'

4. What details tell the reader that Neil's operation was not too serious? ______________

____

5. What action of Dan O'Dowd lets the reader know he is a friendly person? ___________

____

Answers 1. This was done for you. 2. He was in his dressing gown and sitting on the edge of his bed. 3. Neil was aware that Sister had 'worked something out'. OR Neil had seen the old man earlier. 4. He was able to grin (and probably read). 5. He came over to talk to Neil. OR He let Neil read his magazine.

Noting Detail — Spacescape

by Karl Kruszelnicki

When doing research work or projects it is important to get the details right.

Saturn

Saturn is the second of the four gas giants. It is about 120 000 km across. Saturn takes 29.46 years to go round the Sun and, like Jupiter, it spins very rapidly. A day on Saturn lasts for only 10 hours and 39 minutes.

Saturn has a similar structure to the planet Jupiter. Saturn is made up of a solid core, surrounded by a shell of liquid hydrogen. Finally, there is a giant shell of atmosphere. This atmosphere is made up of hydrogen and helium gases, ammonia and small amounts of other gases. Like Jupiter, Saturn seems to be a bubbling cauldron of liquid gases.

Saturn is also similar to Jupiter because the planet gives off more heat than it receives from the Sun. In the same way that steam gives off heat as it turns from gas into liquid, so helium gives off heat. On Saturn, the heat comes from the condensing of helium as it sinks in the atmosphere. Heat is also given off as the core of Saturn contracts, or grows smaller. This heat is the power supply that causes the weather on Saturn, for example, the fierce winds which travel at up to 1700 km an hour near the planet's equator.

While Jupiter has the Great Red Spot, Saturn has the Small Red Spot, which is about 6000 km across. Saturn also has the Great White Spot. This cloud of ammonia crystals seems to appear every 30 years and last appeared on September 24 1990. The Great White Spot always appears in the mid-summer of the northern hemisphere of Saturn. During its last appearance, the Great White Spot very rapidly grew to an oval big enough to swallow three Earths and then stayed the same size for about three weeks. Then Saturn's strong winds began to change the Great White Spot and it became even larger, growing a long tail as it began to stretch around the planet, reaching some 240 km above the cloud tops.

1. Saturn and Jupiter have similarities and differences. Draw lines from 'Similarities' or 'Differences' to match the details from the extract.

	spins rapidly
Similarities	has a solid core
	large cloud of white ammonia crystals
Differences	1700 km/hour winds at the equator
	gives off more heat than it receives

2. When did the Great White Spot last appear on Saturn? ______________________

____

Complete these three sentences about the Great White Spot

3. The Great White Spot appears about every ______________________.

4. The Great White Spot stayed the same size for about ______________________.

5. The Great White Spot is located in ______________________.

Find words in the extract to complete these sentences.

6. Steam gives off ________ as it turns from a gas into a ________.

7. A Saturn day is about _____ hours long but a Saturn year lasts almost ______ years.

8. Two gases found on Saturn are ___________ and ___________ .

Noting Detail — Additional Fables

by Rolf Grunseit

Shadow of the Great Pyramid

The sound of children's laughter came from the wharf down by the Nile River. A middle-aged man was entertaining some local children.

An ocean-going ship had just moored. Workmen were unloading cargo onto waiting camels.

'It's impossible,' the children yelled. 'It's impossible!'

'I can do it!' the man insisted. He held up a sheet of papyrus with a hole in it.

'No! You can't push a camel through that hole,' one boy shouted.

'Watch me, I'll show you!' the man said with a grin. He walked up to the camel and patted it.

'You can't!' the children kept screaming.

The man put his hand through the hole in the papyrus sheet and pushed the camel. 'See? I've pushed the camel through the hole.' The stranger smiled.

The children leapt about, shrieking with laughter. 'That's cheating!' they yelled.

A young man standing nearby laughed with the children. He was a government surveyor. Beside him stood his assistants, carrying his equipment.

The year was 590 BC, the place northern Egypt.

1. Draw a line to match the details that go with each person or group of people.

middle-aged man	with men carrying equipment
young surveyor	thrilled by the trick
local children	entertaining on the wharf

2. Choose the best way to complete this sentence. (tick the correct box)

When the entertainer completed his act the children

☐ were not amused. ☐ couldn't believe their eyes.

☐ thought it was magic. ☐ knew they had been tricked.

3. The incident in the extract happened over 2000 years ago. ☐ True ☐ False

4. The cargo from the ship was being packed onto the back of camels. ☐ True ☐ False

5. The incident in the extract took place in southern Egypt. ☐ True ☐ False

6. The young surveyor was not impressed with the trick. ☐ True ☐ False

7. What did the children think the middle aged man was going to try to do? ____________

____

Noting Detail — Desert Gold

by Mark Butler

The search for Lasseter's Reef

Imagine a small, stocky man addressing a crowd in a shady corner of Sydney's Hyde Park on a humid day in March 1930. He is talking about riches beyond anyone's wildest dreams — his slow, musical voice carries across the park, drawing more and more listeners towards him. As he speaks, he hands out pamphlets to as many members of his swelling audience as he can reach. Soon the audience is eagerly handing the pamphlets around for him.

'I tell you, this continent has a heart of solid gold! I've seen it, touched it! Gold is the basis of all wealth, and the gold I have seen will turn Australia into a wealthy country again. No more Depression — a job for every man, and debt banished forever. Think about it, read the pamphlet, then join with me. My friends, for a small investment you can save the country from ruin and become rich!'

Within minutes of finishing his speech, the man is surrounded by people, all of them offering him money …

This scene is made up, but something like this happened in Sydney in 1930, when Harold Lasseter began telling his amazing story. He told of a 23 kilometre reef of gold he had found in unexplored desert country in central Australia — 'Lasseter's Reef', the richest goldmine in Australia!

It was a story many people wanted to hear in 1930. Australia, as well as England, Europe and the United States of America was in the grip of the Depression, a time when living standards of most people dropped greatly. The Depression meant that Australia could not earn enough from selling minerals, wool and other farm products to pay for the goods we bought from other countries.

1. Tick the box that is **NOT** a characteristic of the Depression.

☐ a time of jobs and hard work ☐ poor people wanting to get rich quickly

☐ the income of Australian was safe because exports were high

☐ Australia was not like any other country during the Depression

2. Tick the boxes that give accurate details about Harold Lasseter.

☐ Lasseter believed he had found a vast reef of gold.

☐ Lasseter needed money to start the gold mining.

☐ Lasseter didn't want anyone to know about his reef.

☐ Lasseter wasn't able to convince people about his find.

3. England was not affected by the Depression. ☐ True ☐ False

4. Before the Depression Australia's wealth depended upon farming. ☐ True ☐ False

5. Before Lasseter's find, mining was of no importance in Australia. ☐ True ☐ False

6. Lasseter made his speech in Hyde Park in Melbourne. ☐ True ☐ False

7. Most people thought that Lasseter's gold story was untrue. ☐ True ☐ False

8. To return to the reef and start mining, Lasseter first needed (money miners farmers information). (circle one word)

9. Lasseter was a persuasive public speaker. Yes / No (circle one)

LIFT-OUT ANSWER SECTION

Answers

Page 1: Finding Facts — Introduction

Indonesia by Lisa Hill
1. is situated on an unstable part of the earth 2. loud bangs 3. (7 o'clock on) 27 August 1883
4. It had exploded. 5. many people were killed.

Page 2: Antarctica by John Collerson
1. about 100 years ago 2. an ancient Greek scholar
3. He sailed right round the world on the Southern Ocean. OR He sailed into Antarctic waters in 1773 but didn't go far enough to see the land.
4. False 5. True 6. False 7. True 8. mariners
9. Blizzards may last for days. The sea can freeze over.

Page 3: Spacescape by Karl Kruszelnicki
1. the winds are very strong. 2. gives off more heat than it receives from the sun. 3. Saturn's weather.
4. True 5. False 6. False

Page 4: Earth First by David Bowden & Jenny Dibley
1. how the production of the product will affect the environment.
2. considers many points before making a purchase. 3. False 4. True 5. eight
6. answers will vary

Page 5: Beowulf's Downfall by Brad Turner
1. Wiglaf and Beowulf 2. get only those items of greatest value. 3. making him the new king.
4. amazement 5. False 6. False 7. False

Page 6: Eyes On The World by David Bolliger
1. If you can't read words — you can still get facts from pictures.
Photographs look like — a little piece of the world.
When you first started to read — words seemed like squiggles on the paper.
2. is about the importance of photographs. 3. False 4. False 5. True 6. answers will vary
7. are both used to tell stories.

Page 7: Finding the Main Idea — Introduction

Perfect Timing by Jeremy Fisher
1. four 2. four 3. two 4. Starting school (The other options are about details.)
5. houses in the street 6. True 7. why there is a big change in Andrew's mood.

Page 8: Land of the Rippling Gold by Una Clarke
1. getting Wendy's leg treated. 2. Wendy blamed herself for the accident.
3. They were barely out of town when the accident happened. 4. Wendy's leg swells up and her parents begin to take her to the doctor. 5. The accident 6. False 7. False 8. True

Page 9: Rainforests by Stephen Jones
1. six 2. The canopy is the powerhouse of the tropical rainforest.
3. Several answers. It is windier/ less humid / sunnier than the canopy.
4. an environment of many levels. 5. the tallest (trees) 6. Features of a rainforest. 7. True
8. False

Page 10: Dream Door of Shinar by Patricia Bernard
1. two
2. Paragraph 1 — leaping through the Door
Paragraph 2 — the Door begins to disappear
Paragraph 3 — changed backyard
3. The strange Door. 4. Paragraph 4 5. Kevin's father followed him through the Door.
6. True 7. True 8. concerned

Page 11: Perfect Timing by Jeremy Fisher
1. eight 2. Then the band finished their set. 3. The award winning band. 4. True 5. False
6. True 7. False 8. thrilled

Page 12: Spacescape by Karl Kruszelnicki
1. The size of Saturn. 2. structure of Saturn. 3. Great White Spot of Saturn. 4. False 5. True
6. True 7. Saturn also has the Great White Spot. 8. supporting detail.

Page 13: Making Inferences — Introduction

The Crystal Key by Pamela O'Connor
1. Several answers: Chris doesn't answer. The children were going deeper into the strange tunnel.
2. Joel remains calm. 3. Possible answers: Chris gasps/Chris doesn't answer/ Joel hisses 'Don't move.'
4. it is deep and dark.

Page 14: Dream Door Of Shinar by Patricia Bernard
1. Several answers. The queen ant flung the loaf onto the ground. Thurt was fighting the ants with an axe. The ant had its front legs on Cloud's shoulders and its middle legs on Cloud's waist.
2. The boys carried flaming torches. 3. Cloud 4. Cloud was within easy reach of the queen.
5. Thurt 6. Thurt led the attack on the ants. 7. True.

Page 15: Through the web by Ellen Robertson
1. Lyndell 2. reacts without getting all the facts./ has a vivid imagination. 3. practical.
4. False 5. False 6. To find out how dangerous the spider was. 7. Lyndell's habit of exaggerating.

Page 16: Night of the Muttonbirds by Mary Small
1. found their nesting place. 2. calm 3. The houses are kept warm with wood fires. 4. True
5. True 6. curtained the rising moon

Page 17: Using Context Clues — Introduction

The Crystal Key by Pamela O'Connor
1. the children own many things. 2. Often, because Mrs Kelly didn't feel like another argument.
3. fashion sense 4. False

Page 18: Courageous Crew by Kathleen Allanby
1. They stretched the rabbit skins over wire frames and hung them on nails. / They tacked out the possum skins flat against the outside wall to dry.
2. had seen the hen with the chickens. 3. a clear (fine) day 4. timid
5. a hen with a brood of chickens. 6. False 7. False

Page 19: Do They Play Marbles On Mars? by Margaret McAlister
1. a teacher. 2. it was better than picking up papers. 3. pretending to be bored by Michael's answer.
4. Cheryl and Michael did not get on very well. They both did things to upset the other.
5. Michael looked at the floor because he was embarrassed that he had to apologise. (other reasons possible)
6. meanly 7. True

Page 20: Courageous Crew by Kathleen Allanby
1. It probably happened many years ago because Abe was a blacksmith.
2. let anyone they meet know what is happening. 3. uncaring 4. bored 5. aching 6. True
7. True 8. Abe and Mr Mick 9. very clean.

Page 21: Drawing Conclusions — Introduction

The Miners Rest by Robert L. Muddyman
1. She keeps calm. She suggests a solution to the problem.
2. They had spent some time (stated in Council letter) and money renovating the Miners Rest.
3. concerned 4. Unexpected Letter
5. The letter was friendly/formal. George and Terrie had had some time to complete the work. (see Council letter)

Page 22: Do They Play Marbles On Mars? by Margaret McAlister
1. (C) 2. Cheryl pulled the rope high and turned it fast.
3. (a 'big shot') He let himself be taunted by Cheryl. He thought he was good at skipping.
4. She was a slave driver. She was a mean bully. 5. False

Page 23: Australia's Unwritten History by Oodgeroo Noonuccal
1. Children, playing on the beach, recognised Gwondo. AND Gwondo trains dolphins to chase fish close to the shore.
2. hunting/helping to feed the tribe 3. wanted/The children had been mourning for too long. 4. True

Page 24: Technology For The Environment by Mike Callaghan & Peter Knapp
1. People plough the soil to grow crops. There is too much crop irrigation. Forests are being removed on steep slopes.
2. Trees hold the topsoil in place. 3. a result of poor farm management 4. False
5. more trees are planted. 6. True 7. False 8. True.

Page 25: Noting Detail — Introduction

Forbidden Territory by Kathleen Allanby
1. This was done for you. 2. He was in his dressing gown and sitting on the edge of his bed.
3. Neil was aware that Sister had 'worked something out'. OR Neil had seen the old man earlier.
4. He was able to grin (and probably read).
5. He came over to talk to Neil. OR He let Neil read his magazine.

Page 26: Spacescape by Karl Kruszelnicki
1.
Similarities — spins rapidly
Similarities — has a solid core
Differences — large cloud of white ammonia crystals
Differences — 1700 km/hour winds at the equator
Similarities — gives off more heat than it receives
2. September 24 1990 3. 30 years 4. three weeks 5. the northern hemisphere of Saturn.
6. Steam gives off heat as it turns from a gas into a liquid.
7. A Saturn day is about 10 hours long but a Saturn year lasts almost 30 years. 8. hydrogen and helium

Page 27: Additional Fables by Rolf Grunseit
1. middle aged man — entertaining on the wharf
young surveyor — with men carrying equipment
local children — thrilled by the trick
2. knew they had been tricked. 3. True 4. True 5. False 6. False
7. That he was going to make the camel go through the hole in the papyrus.

Page 28: Desert Gold by Mark Butler
1. a time of jobs and hard work
2. Lasseter believed he had found a vast reef of gold. Lasseter needed money to start the gold mining.
3. False 4. False (farming and mining) 5. False 6. False 7. False 8. money 9. Yes

Page 29: Following Directions — Introduction

1. 7 steps 2. six 3. four to six people 4. Cut each chicken wing into 2 pieces 5. Wait until the oil is hot 6. crushed, grated 7. 30 minutes

Page 30: How to Grow Crystals
1. four 2. twelve 3. Many examples: supersaturated, solution, copper sulphate
4. saucepan and a stove 5. Making the solution 6. True 7. True
8. Pour 150mL of water into the beaker.

Page 31: Exploring and Making a Packet Cake Recipe
1. four 2. a wooden spoon 3. oven or a microwave
4. Preheat gas or electric oven to 180°C and grease and flour cake pan. 5. 35–40 minutes
6. (polyunsaturated) vegetable oil 7. springs back when lightly touched in the centre. 8. False
9. True 10. False (it should cool for 5 minutes first) 10. batter

Page 32: Martians Are Really Nice People a play by Dianne Bates & Bill Condon
1. 14 2. three 3. play should look (appear). (other variations possible) 4. a suit with a bow tie
5. True 6. False 7. tea cup 8. a desk and chair.

Page 33: Understanding Questions — Introduction

Spacecape by Karl Kruszelnicki

1. The core of Uranus consists of iron and silicon.
2. The core of Uranus is about 14 000 km in diameter. The weather on Uranus does not change very much. The layer above the core is a thick layer of ice and gases.
3. False 4. of the giant gas planets 5. larger 6. Answers will vary.

Page 34: That's a job for me! by Ross Pearce

1. **Mark**	**Ricky**
stolen goods	football skills
robberies	team
details	sports car
investigate	professional
belongings	game

2. Mark 3. Mark 4. Education officer

5. Mark says that most children — who run off, turn up again.
   It is important to Ricky to — have money to pay the bills.
   It is important for Mark to — help people improve their skills.

6. helpful 7. answers will vary 8. the police

Page 35: Understanding Questions — Cloze

Spacescape by Karl Kruszelnicki
Uranus is tilted and lies on its side. This means that the north and south poles on Uranus do not point straight up and (1) **down** — one points towards the Sun, while the other pole points away from the Sun. The current scientific theory is that a colossal impact with a large object must have tipped Uranus on its (2) **side**. Scientists believe that this must have (3) **happened** quite early in the history of Uranus. Uranus' satellites go around the equator of the planet, so they must have formed after the big impact that caused Uranus to tilt.

Australia's Unwritten History by Oodgeroo Noonuccal
Gwondo was the trainer of dogs. He would go out every (4) **day** with his dogs to teach them how to ambush animals so all the tribe could eat. He had an elongated head, and his dark hair was interrupted by a crest of white hair that shone in the sunlight. It was just like the crest on the (5) **head** of a cockatoo, only Gwondo's crest was white.

Wherever Gwondo went, his (6) **tribe** could see him away in the distance on the hills, because his white hair would shine in the sunlight. The tribal elders would say to their children, 'See, there is Gwondo and his dogs, searching for food for us all.' Gwondo went hunting every day and he always came back to the camp with much food for his tribe. And all were very happy.

7. Sequencing
   3 Then her father had hurried off to work with milk dripping from his tie.
   1 Sitting in class, Yvonne remembered something funny and began laughing.
   4 When Ms Younger, the teacher, stopped reading she suddenly realised that the whole class was looking at her in amusement.
   2 She couldn't shut the picture of her father with his tie in his porridge, out of her mind.

Page 36: Antarctica by John Collerson

1. (D) been polluted mostly around the bases.
2. (C) taken back to the country it came from.
3. (A) saved for research.
4. 1 Antarctica was free of pollution.
   4 Airstrips were built to improve transport.
   2 People set up bases in Antarctica.
   3 At first, researchers did not worry about pollution.

Page 37: Understanding Paragraphs — Introduction

Zeppo by Virginia King from *Through the web and other stories*

1. a) 5 b) 2 c) 5 d) 4 e) 2 2. along the road 3. at the front gate
4. It is a dramatic event for Joanne. 5. Joanne

Page 38: Understanding Paragraphs — 2

Framing Ned Kelly by Louise Martin-Chew

> Sidney Nolan was born on 22 April 1917 at Carlton, Victoria. His parents were living in a town called Ngambie, in north-eastern Victoria before he was born. This area is known as 'Kelly country' because Ned Kelly and his gang lived and roamed through it in the 1870s. //
> Soon after Sidney was born, he and his parents moved to a bayside Melbourne suburb called St Kilda. Here Sidney became an artist and St Kilda often appeared in his paintings. //
> St Kilda was a lively place in the summer; crowded with holiday-makers. However, in the winter it was cold, bleak and eerily empty.

2. **Do They Play Marbles On Mars?** by Margaret McAlister

> Cheryl smirked. I glared at her. Cheryl had done much worse things to me. Mrs Jackson hardly ever caught her. I should have just dobbed Cheryl in for letting that match box full of ants loose in my lunch box. //
> 'Go ahead, Michael,' said Mrs Jackson. 'Unless you'd like to pick up papers for a week.'//
> I thought about it for a moment. It would almost be worth it to choose the papers, but then I thought of Cheryl following me around all week yelling insults while I picked up the rubbish. Then I would be forced to stuff some dirty, sticky iceblock wrappers down her T-shirt . . . and then I would get two weeks of picking up papers . . . //
> 'Sorry,' I muttered, looking at the floor.

3. **Indonesia** by Lisa Hill

> Indonesian people have a strong sense of their own regional or tribal identity. They describe themselves first as Bataks, Balinese, Sudanese, Irianese, Minangkabau and so on. However, Javanese culture is dominant because the Javanese also led the struggle for independence and because the central government is on Java. //
> The first leader of independent Indonesia was President Sukarno. He understood the importance of using symbols to develop unity amongst his different peoples. //
> He chose the mythical bird, Garuda, for the state crest. Garuda was the powerful sun bird ridden by Prince Vishnu in Hindu mythology, and it was the symbol of the powerful old Javanese kingdom of Majapahit. Although the Hindu religion has now mostly been replaced by Islam throughout Indonesia, Hindu stories and dance are still a very important part of Indonesia culture. Garuda is also the name of the Indonesian international airline.

4. **Do They Play Marbles On Mars?** by Margaret McAlister

> 'I saw that, Michael!' said Mrs Jackson. Come out here!' //
> 'What?' I tried to look innocent. 'What did I do?' //
> Mrs Jackson sighed. She looked up at the ceiling then back at me. 'Apologise to Cheryl.' //
> Now, that was *really* heavy. It was only a bit of screwed-up paper. Nobody ever died from being hit on the head by an old maths test.

Page 39: Relevant and Irrelevant Information — Introduction

Indonesia by Lisa Hill

1. Indonesia is an interesting place for scientists to study fossils. 2. destroyed an island

Page 40: Night of the Muttonbirds by Mary Small

1. The view of the mountains impressed Matthew. Looking back at the house brought tears to Matthew's eyes.
2. irate, cruel, content 3. deserted, natural 4. Matthew is about to leave home. 5. Shelley

Page 41: Desert Gold by Mark Butler
1. It was decided to use local Aborigines as guides. An airstrip was planned for Yayai Creek.
2. wary, spiteful, disorganised, timid 3. harsh, without services, mountainous, difficult
4. to find a reef (of gold). 5. False 6. False (aeroplane) 7. True 8. True

Page 42: Technology For The Environment by Mike Callaghan & Peter Knapp
1. ploughing the land; increased numbers of grazing animals
2. they all help to remove vegetation and leave the soil open to the effects of wind and rain.
3. (B) could take over a thousand years. 4. irrigation, pastures, crops, clearing
5. (B) Soil erosion is balanced by soil build up. (D) Much soil ends up at the bottom of the ocean.
6. True

Page 43: Fact and Opinion — Introduction
Shaping the news by John D. Fitzgerald
1. opinion 2. fact 3. fact 4. fact 5. True 6. False (3 methods are used)

Page 44: Fact and Opinion — 2
The Thunder God by David Shapiro
1. Fei was a fine student. 2. True

Framing Ned Kelly by Louise Martin-Chew
3. Days off school may have helped Sidney to develop an interest in painting. 4. dismay 5. False

Page 45: Antarctica by John Collerson
1. Antarctica is a uniquely beautiful part of the world. 2. False 3. True 4. False 5. True
6. taken back to the country it came from. 7. Answers will vary.
8. Possible answers: library, government services, nature films

Page 46: Eyes of the world by David Bolliger
1. The council seemed more worried about bad press than someone being attacked.
2. True 3. newspaper, opinion 4. True
5. (A) Miller's photo appealed to the reader's sense of fear. 6. True 7. gives the impression

Page 47: Understanding Persuasion — Introduction
1. yourself (boy or girl) 2. We will put you on the road to stardom! 3. True 4. No 5. No

Page 48: Earth First by David Bowden & Jenny Dibley
1. entice (persuade) people (consumers) to buy products (some of which they may not need).
2. assumed the reader is an intelligent person. 3. persuade people to buy.
4. Answers will vary — example: Barbie/Ken 5. he/she can now understand how advertising is used.

Page 49: Desert Gold by Mark Butler
1. Gold is the basis of all wealth.
2. (A) they have a chance to be wealthy; (C) that Lasseter wants each person to be part of his plans.
3. excited 4. riches are readily available 5. False 6. False

Page 50: Earth First by David Bowden & Jenny Dibley
1. make the reader think about the subject.
2. persuade the buyer that there is a need to purchase the item quickly
3. True 4. False 5. Answers will vary. 6. speaking to the reader in a very personal, friendly manner.
7. make you more suspicious of advertising.

Page 51: Understanding and Using a Table of Contents
Australia's Inland Sea by Dr T. Flannery & P. Kendall
1. page 54 2. Animals of the inland sea 3. True 4. False 5. True 6. Index

Page 52: Homeland Australia by Michael Dugan
1. page 57 2. page 46 3. Multicultural Australia 4. Index 5. False 6. True 7. nine
8. Glossary 9. front, back 10. front

Page 53: Understanding and Using an Index — Introduction
1. page 33 2. three 3. paper 4. False 5. True 6. p. 32 (and onto p. 33).

Page 54: Shaping the News by John D. Fitzgerald
1. page 5 or 14 2. illustration 3. page 38 4. Murphy 5. True 6. False 7. True
8. The word **The** is not the important word. 9. 3

Page 55: Using Timetables — Introduction
1. 6:30 2. 6:45 3. holidays 4. ten
5. Auckland at 6 pm 6. False 7. False 8. True 9. three

Page 56: Using Timetables — TV guide
1. ABN 2. 1 hour 3. No 4. ABN 5. repeat 6. 8:30 7. Night Train OR Ozone
8. False 9. False 10. True 11. Pet hotline 12. Pacific Post 13. Saturday, 22 January
14. Holiday Line
15. 3 Wildlife Park
1 Sky Devils
4 Our Street
2 Lost in Space

Page 57: Understanding Maps — Introduction
1. west 2. south 3. east 4. 300 km 5. Solo OR Brantas, 6. ten 7. Ci Julang 8. Pacitan

Page 58: The Islands of Manihiki (Cook Islands)
1. a) north (or north east) b) east c) south 4. reef 5. Ngaka 6. Ill 7. lagoon 8. 9km
9. True

Page 59: Understanding Graphs and Charts — Introduction
1. True 2. New South Wales 3. True 4. True 5. Western Australia or Northern Territory
6. farming

Page 60: Spacescape by Karl Kruszelnicki
1. five 2. Mercury and Venus 3. Pluto
4. Pluto Phobos
Mars Titan
Jupiter Charon
Saturn Oberon
Uranus Ganymede
5. False 6. True 7. 2:Neptune 1:Earth 4: Saturn 3:Uranus

Following Directions — Introduction

If we want to know how to do something we have to follow **a procedure** or, as some people say, **follow directions**. You may have books at home that tell you how to do things. Books with many sets of directions are called **manuals**. Some people have manuals for making repairs. They might be called **how-to** books.

Some directions are simple. A machine at a ferry terminal has **instructions** on how to purchase a ticket. We call each part of the directions (instructions) **steps**. People follow directions nearly every day of their lives.

Read the following set of simple instructions; from *What's Cooking* by Kerri Bingle, David Bowden and Jenny Dibley.

Honey Chicken Wings ← ***The aim** (what you will make)*

Serves 4 to 6 people ← *How many people you will be catering for.*

Ingredients ← *Often called the materials needed.*

1 kg chicken wings
½ teaspoon grated ginger
1 to 2 cloves of crushed garlic
3 tablespoons honey
3 tablespoons peanut oil
⅓ cup soy sauce

Method ← ***The steps** (or directions) you must follow.*

1. Cut each chicken wing into 2 pieces.
2. Pour peanut oil into wok.
3. When the oil is hot, place the chicken pieces into the oil and cook for about 6 to 8 minutes or until the chicken is browned.
4. Add the other ingredients and stir well.
5. Reduce the heat to low. Place a cover over the wok.
6. Stir the chicken frequently making sure that the glaze does not burn.
7. Let the chicken simmer for about 30 minutes. ← *concluding step*

Honey chicken wings can be served at the beginning of the meal as a snack, or as the main meal with fluffy rice. Try using chopsticks. ← *concluding statement*

1. How many steps are there in making honey chicken wings? _________

2. How many different ingredients do you need to make honey chicken wings? _____

3. This recipe makes enough honey chicken wings for _____ people.

4. After getting the ingredients what is the first thing to do? _________________________

5. Before putting the chicken pieces into the wok you should _______________________.

6. The garlic is __________ and the ginger is _________ .

7. The chicken wings must simmer for ______ minutes.

Answers 1. 7, 2. 6, 3. 4 to 6, 4. Cut each chicken wing into 2 pieces, 5. Wait until the oil is hot, 6. crushed, grated, 7. 30 minutes

Following Directions — How to Grow Crystals

Science experiments have their own way of giving instructions. They often use **scientific language**. For most science experiments it is essential to get the **equipment** and **materials** ready before you start.

The equipment and materials you require are usually listed in the order needed.

The directions in an experiment are often called the **method**.

How to Grow Crystals

What you need

2 polystyrene foam cups
Cotton thread
paperclips
1 tripod
1 heat-proof mat
1 bunsen burner
Copper sulphate
150 mL water (approximately)
1 teaspoon
1 heat proof glass beaker
1 stirring rod (or heat resistant plastic spoon)
1 potholder

Note: A saucepan and a stove can be substituted for the beaker, tripod and bunsen burner.

Steps

Part 1. Preparing the equipment

1. Attach a paper clip to a piece of thread about 30 cm long.
2. Suspend the paper clip into a foam cup.
3. Take the second foam cup and cut away the upper third. This is used to hold the thread firmly and as a lid for the first cup.
4. Set up the bunsen burner and the tripod with the heat proof mat.

Part 2. Making the solution

1. Pour 150mL of water into the beaker.
2. Add copper sulphate to the water one teaspoon at the time while stirring to dissolve it.
3. Keep adding copper sulphate until no more will dissolve and some is left on the bottom.
4. Place the beaker on the bunsen burner and light the burner.
5. Gently heat the solution until all copper sulphate is dissolved.
6. Continue to add copper sulphate, half a teaspoon at a time, until no more will dissolve.
   The solution is now **supersaturated**.
7. Turn off the heat.

Now you are ready to grow crystals in your polystyrene foam cup.

1. How many steps are there in **preparing the equipment**? ____________

2. How many items should you get before starting the experiment? ____________

3. Give two scientific words used in the directions. ____________, ____________

4. What can be used instead of a bunsen burner and beaker? ____________

5. The second part of the instructions is called ____________.

6. This experiment can be done without proper scientific equipment. ☐ True ☐ False

7. Dissolving enough copper sulphate is the main purpose of Part 2. ☐ True ☐ False

8. After getting the materials and equipment ready, the first step in the experiment is to

____________.

Following Directions — Exploring and Making a Packet Cake Recipe

Have a careful look at this cake mix box. What sort of information do we find on packet cake mixes? Here is a recipe from a White Wings packet.

WHITE WINGS CARROT CAKE MIX

Easy directions

Preheat gas or electric oven to 180°C (350°F).
Grease and flour cake pan, or lightly grease a non stick-pan.

Do not use an electric mixer.

MIX in a bowl, Cake Mix, 1 egg, ⅔ cup water,
60g (2 oz) polyunsaturated margarine, (or ⅓ cup polyunsaturated vegetable oil) with a wooden spoon.

BEAT only until ingredients are combined (approximately 30 seconds).

BAKE for 40–45 minutes in a 22cm x 11cm loaf pan or 35–40 minutes in a 20cm ring pan. Cake is baked if it springs back when lightly touched in the centre. Allow cake to cool in pan for 5–8 minutes before inverting onto a cake cooler.

Directions for a 600w microwave Oven

Place Cake Mix, 1 egg, ⅔ cup water, 60g polyunsaturated margarine, 1 tablespoon polyunsaturated vegetable oil into a bowl and beat with a wooden spoon for 30 seconds.

Pour batter into a greased 2 litre microwave safe container, microwave on high for 6 minutes (if oven does not have a turntable, rotate container 1/4 turn every 2 minutes). Allow cake to cool for 5 minutes before inverting.

Note: As microwave ovens vary, time given may need adjusting to your particular oven.

1. How many different ingredients are needed to make this carrot cake? ______________

2. What should you use to mix the ingredients? ______________

3. The carrot cake can be cooked in an ____________ or a ____________ .

4. Before mixing the ingredients you should first ______________________________.
Find the missing words for each of these sentences.

5. Carrot cake mix should be baked for ____________ minutes in a 20cm ring pan.

6. Instead of using margarine you could use ______________ .

7. Find the correct ending for this sentence. The cake is baked when it

☐ is inverted onto a cake cooler. ☐ has been in the oven for 35 minutes.

☐ turns a light brown on top. ☐ springs back when lightly touched in the centre.

8. The best way to beat a carrot cake mix is with an electric beater. ☐ True ☐ False

9. The pan used for baking the cake should be greased. ☐ True ☐ False

10. When the cake is cooked it is ready to be eaten. ☐ True ☐ False

11. In the microwave instruction the mixture (cake mix, egg, water) is called a ________.

Following Directions — Martians Are Really Nice People

a play by Dianne Bates & Bill Condon from *Stagestruck!*

When putting on a play we also follow directions.

Staging
The stage should be split into three different sets. Set one is the TV studio with a desk, behind which Katrina French-fry sits. Set two is the Speelbug's lounge room (complete with television set and a beanbag or armchair). The third set is for the outdoor TV broadcast. A painted backdrop will help create an outdoor atmosphere for the third set.

Costumes and props
Costumes will add brightness and fun to this play's presentation. Irene Greenbean, Tutan, Khaman, Saspa, Rilla and Mum all wear green. General Plan is dressed in khaki-coloured clothing, and is liberally covered with medals and ribbons. Johnny Ondispot is dressed in a suit and bow tie, while Les Toro wears overalls. Katrina French-fry should be dressed 'smartly' while Steve should be dressed casually. Megan can also be dressed casually.
Additional props for this play include:

- ☆ a microphone
- ☆ a video camera (can be real or improvised)
- ☆ a credit card
- ☆ a note
- ☆ a newspaper
- ☆ a coin
- ☆ a pen and notebook
- ☆ a book titled: 'Martians Are Really Nice People'

Music and sound effects
Music from the film *Shaft* can be used to great effect in this play.

Characters

KATRINA FRENCH-FRY
GENERAL STAN PLAN
IRENE GREENBEAN
MEGAN SPEELBUG
SASPA
JOHNNY ONDISPOT
CAMERA PERSON
STEVE SPEELBUG
TUTAN
RILLA
LES TORO
STATION ASSISTANT
MRS SPEELBUG (MUM)
KHARMAN

1. How many characters are in the play? __________

2. How many different sets are needed for this play? __________

3. The section Costumes and Props suggests how the ______________________________.

4. Johnny Ondispot should wear ______________________________.

5. Music from *Shaft* would make the play more interesting. ☐ True ☐ False

6. It is essential to have a real video camera for this play. ☐ True ☐ False

7. Which of the following is NOT a prop for the play: **pen, coin, tea cup**. (circle one word)

8. Tick the box that completes this sentence. In the TV studio set there should be

☐ an armchair or beanbag. ☐ a desk and chair.

Understanding Questions — Introduction

In your comprehension exercises you will get many different types of questions. Different types of questions are used to see just how well you read and understand what you have read. You will get a number of different types of questions in this book.

Types of questions:

true–false questions (yes–no)
multiple choice questions
short answer questions
full sentence answer questions
matching exercises
sentence completing exercises
sequencing questions
labelling exercises
cloze exercises (filling in blanks)

- Questions that want you to **find information** may begin with how, when where or what. Sometimes you will be asked to give **names** or make **lists**.
- Questions that want you to **give a reason** will often begin with why.
- Some questions may ask you to **give an opinion**. For these questions you have to have your own ideas. These questions may ask you to **give answers in your own words**.
- Other questions may ask you to **search and find** information, especially in factual texts.

Read this extract from *Spacescape* by Karl Kruszelnicki and answer the questions.

> Although Uranus is the third of the gas giants, it is quite different to the other planets. Uranus is about four times the size of Earth and has a solid core made up of iron and silicates. This solid core is about 14 000 km in diameter, just a little larger than our whole planet. Above the solid core is a 9000 km thick layer of ice and various gases (mostly hydrogen and helium, with a little methane).
>
> There doesn't seem to be much visible weather happening on Uranus and the temperature from the poles to the equator is almost constant, changing to become only two degrees warmer or colder.

1. What does the core of Uranus consist of? (**full sentence answer**) ____________________

____

2. Draw a line to **match** these sentence beginnings with their right endings.

The core of Uranus is	a thick layer of ice and gases.
The weather on Uranus	about 14 000 km in diameter.
The layer above the core is	does not change very much.

3. Uranus is smaller than Earth. ☐ True ☐ False

4. Complete this sentence. Uranus is the third ____________________.

5. The core of Uranus is (larger than smaller than the same as) the Earth's core. (circle one answer)

6. Would you like to live on Uranus? ______ What is your reason? (no written answer required)

Answers 1. iron and silicon, 2. The core of Uranus is about 14 000 km in diameter. The weather on Uranus does not change very much. The layer above the core is a thick layer of ice and gases. 3. False, 4. of the giant gas planets. 5. larger than, 6. Answers will vary.

Understanding Questions — That's a job for me!

by Ross Pearce

Read these reports by people who enjoy their work.

Mark, The Policeman

Why work? To get enough money to travel, to buy a house, to pay the bills. That's not to say I don't get enjoyment out of my job, but my main reason to work is so that I can earn the money to do the things I want to do in my life.

I suppose everyone knows a little of what a policeman does. If your house has been broken into and your belongings stolen, who do you call? No, not the ghost busters, you call the police! We go around to people's homes and take the details of robberies and hopefully, recover the stolen goods. We also answer calls where people are having arguments and investigate stolen cars. At our station we also receive calls from distraught parents whose children have run off. Usually the children turn up unharmed, but children should always make sure their parents know where they are.

Ricky, The Education Officer and Footballer

In my work as an education officer I help people improve their lives and that's really important to me. I also play professional football because I love the game. I enjoy being part of a team and I get a lot of pleasure from using the football skills I have developed over the years.

The financial rewards from both jobs are certainly welcome too. I've just bought a new sports car and it's great. I enjoy the things I can buy with the money I earn from work.

1. These words go with **Mark** or **Ricky**. Can you put them in the right box? (Search and find)

football skills	team	stolen goods	robberies	details
sports car	investigate	belongings	professional	game

Mark ______ ______ ______ ______ ______ ______

Ricky ______ ______ ______ ______ ______ ______

Write short answers (one or two words) for questions 2 to 4.

2. Whose work takes him into people's houses? ______

3. Who likes to spend his money on travel? ______

4. What else is Ricky other than a footballer? ______

5. Draw a line to **match** these sentence beginnings with their right endings.

Mark says that most children	help people improve their skills.
It is important to Ricky to	have money to pay the bills.
It is important for Mark to	who run off, turn up again.

6. Mark and Ricky could be described as being (lazy helpful greedy). (Circle one word)

7. In **your opinion** who has the best job? ______ because ______.

8. If a house is broken into you should call

☐ ghost busters. ☐ the police. (tick one box)

Understanding Questions — Cloze Exercises and Sequencing

In **cloze exercises** you have to select the best word to fill (**close**) the space. To do cloze exercises well you should read the title of the extract, the whole extract and look at any pictures. When you have completed the exercise, read it through again from the beginning to make sure it makes good sense.

Read these extracts and answer the questions. (From the options for each number, shade the correct **letter** to complete the sentence. Don't write in the space.)

Spacescape by Karl Kruszelnicki

Uranus is tilted and lies on its side. This means that the north and south poles on Uranus do not point straight up and (1)__________ — one points towards the Sun, while the other pole points away from the Sun. The current scientific theory is that a colossal impact with a large object must have tipped Uranus on its (2)__________. Scientists believe that this must have (3)__________quite early in the history of Uranus. Uranus' satellites go around the equator of the planet, so they must have formed after the big impact that caused Uranus to tilt.

1. (A) down (B) across (C) over (D) around

2. (A) back (B) edge (C) side (D) end

3. (A) happened (B) started (C) broken (D) stopped

This time you can write the answers on the lines in the spaces.

Australia's Unwritten History by Oodgeroo Noonuccal

Gwondo was the trainer of dogs. He would go out every (4)____________ with his dogs to teach them how to ambush animals so all the tribe could eat. He had an elongated head, and his dark hair was interrupted by a crest of white hair that shone in the sunlight. It was just like the crest on the (5)____________ of a cockatoo, only Gwondo's crest was white.

Wherever Gwondo went, his (6) ____________ could see him away in the distance on the hills, because his white hair would shine in the sunlight. The tribal elders would say to their children, 'See, there is Gwondo and his dogs, searching for food for us all.' Gwondo went hunting every day and he always came back to the camp with much food for his tribe. And all were very happy.

4. (A) day (B) night (C) time (D) year **5.** (A) hair (B) tail (C) head (D) back

6. (A) dogs (B) animals (C) cockatoos (D) tribe

7. In this exercise you must put the sentences in their correct **sequence** so that the extract makes sense. Write the numbers 2, 3, and 4 in the boxes. The first one has been done to help you get started. When you have number the squares, read it aloud (quietly) to see if your **sequence** makes sense.

- [ ] Then her father had hurried off to work with milk dripping from his tie.
- [1] Sitting in class, Yvonne remembered something funny and began laughing.
- [ ] When Ms Younger, the teacher, stopped reading she suddenly realised that the whole class was looking at her in amusement.
- [ ] She couldn't shut the picture of her father, with his tie in his porridge, out of her mind.

Understanding Questions — Antarctica

by John Collerson

Read the passage and try the **multiple choice questions**. Circle the correct letter.

Antarctica is a uniquely beautiful part of the world whose fragile environment is a delicate balance of natural forces and living creatures. It is very little disturbed by human contact and almost completely free from pollution. There are different ideas about what we should do with Antarctica. Many scientists and others feel that, apart from scientific research, it should be left alone. If it is preserved we can learn a lot about the rest of the world from it. Bubbles of air tapped in the ice and the nature of the ice itself can tell scientists about the earth's atmosphere and climate at various times in the past and so changes in the earth's climate, pollution levels and the greenhouse effect are able to be seen. If Antarctica itself becomes polluted, the usefulness of this measure will be lost. Antarctica also plays an important part in the control of our weather and climate. Too much interference could upset these benefits. Other people say that we should open up Antarctica for tourism or use it as a source of food and mineral resources for the world's needs.

Since people have been going to the Antarctic the problem of pollution has arisen. Although there is little pollution in the continent as a whole, a few bases and expeditions have polluted some areas. In Antarctica rubbish does not decompose as it does in warmer climates and it is not possible to bury anything as the ice-free ground is mainly solid rock. So rubbish just accumulates or is blown about by the wind — even scrap metal. There have also been oil spills and dumping of rubbish at sea by ships. Today there is better control and some rubbish has to be taken back to the home country. Another set of problems comes with the transport needs of the bases, especially the building of airstrips, which can damage the environment greatly. These problems will be magnified if too many people continue to go to Antarctica. So we must face the question: what should we do with Antarctica?

1. Since people have been going to Antarctica it has
(A) become very polluted.
(B) remained pollution free.
(C) not suffered the pollution of the nearby seas.
(D) been polluted mostly around the bases.

2. To overcome any pollution problems rubbish is
(A) dumped from ships into the ocean.
(B) buried in ground that is not frozen.
(C) taken back to the country it came from.
(D) allowed to blow away in the wind.

3. Scientists believe that Antarctica should be
(A) saved for research.
(B) used to dump rubbish.
(C) mined for its mineral wealth.
(D) opened up for tourists.

4. Write the numbers 1 to 4 in the boxes to show the **sequence** of events in Antarctica.

☐ Antarctica was free of pollution.

☐ Airstrips were built to improve transport.

☐ People set up bases in Antarctica.

☐ At first, researchers did not worry about pollution.

Understanding Paragraphs — Introduction

We had an early look at paragraphs in **Finding the Main Idea**. Read page 7 again.

Paragraphs indicate the introduction of new circumstances or people into the writing.

New paragraphs usually show the introduction of:

- a change of ideas or characters,
- a change of place/setting,
- a change of time,
- a change of action (what's happening),
- a change of speakers in conversation.

Each new paragraph starts on a new line. In some writing it is **indented** (about 1cm in).

Paragraphs usually contain:

- a topic sentence (see **Finding the Main Idea**),
- other sentences providing supporting detail,
- two to ten sentences.

Single sentence paragraphs are used for effect (impact) or in speech/conversations.

Read the extract from **Zeppo** by Virginia King from *Through the web and other stories*.

There was an eerie silence in the street as Joanne walked home from school. Puzzled, she looked around. Everything seemed normal. Some kids were chasing each other up ahead, and a truck rumbled noisily along the road. It was an ordinary afternoon, so why did everything seem stiller than usual?

Joanne dismissed the feeling of disquiet and began to plan her afternoon. She decided to take Zeppo for his walk before settling down to hours of homework.

She looked to the familiar old red gate and stopped. Something was wrong. The hollow of dirt underneath it was empty. She dropped her bag on the footpath, pushed open the gate and rushed around to the back door. Bursting into the kitchen, Joanne shouted at her mother, 'Where's Zeppo?'

'Oh, Joanne,' whispered her mother. 'We should have done something about that gate. He got under it again and out on the road. The driver took him to the vet, but —'

'He's dead, isn't he?' Joanne's voice was harsh.

1. Write the number of sentences in each paragraph.

a) Paragraph 1 ________ b) Paragraph 2 ________ c) Paragraph 3 __________

d) Paragraph 4 ________ e) Paragraph 5 ________

2. Where does the action in paragraph 1 take place? __________________

3. Where does the action in paragraph 3 take place? __________________

4. Why is paragraph 5 so short? (tick one)

☐ It is a dramatic event for Joanne. ☐ The story is getting more interesting.

☐ Joanne is confused. ☐ The story has gone to a new setting (change of place).

☐ There has been a change in speakers.

5. The main character in paragraph 3 is (Joanne the mother Zeppo).

Answers 1. a) 5 b) 2 c) 5 d) 4 e) 2, 2. along the road, 3. at the front gate, 4. It is a dramatic event for Joanne. 5. Joanne

Understanding Paragraphs — 2

On this page you have four exercises in which you have to select where the paragraph breaks should be. The extracts have been copied without the breaks in place. Slashes have been inserted at the end of sentences. Use a coloured pencil or highlighter to colour the slash where one paragraph ends and a new paragraph begins.

1. Highlight two places in this extract where new paragraphs should begin. (The first one has been done (with a double slash — //) to help you).
Framing Ned Kelly by Louise Martin-Chew

Sidney Nolan was born on 22 April 1917 at Carlton, Victoria. His parents were living in a town called Ngambie, in north-eastern Victoria before he was born. This area is known as 'Kelly country' because Ned Kelly and his gang lived and roamed through it in the 1870s. **//** Soon after Sidney was born, he and his parents moved to a bayside Melbourne suburb called St Kilda. / Here Sidney became an artist and St Kilda often appeared in his paintings. / St Kilda was a lively place in the summer; crowded with holiday-makers. / However, in the winter it was cold, bleak and eerily empty.

2. In this extract from *Do They Play Marbles On Mars?* by Margaret McAlister, highlight three places where new paragraphs should start.

Cheryl smirked. / I glared at her. / Cheryl had done much worse things to me. / Mrs Jackson hardly ever caught *her*. / I should have just dobbed Cheryl in for letting that match box full of ants loose in my lunch box. / 'Go ahead, Michael,' said Mrs Jackson. 'Unless you'd like to pick up papers for a week.'/ I thought about it for a moment. It would almost be worth it to choose the papers, but then I thought of Cheryl following me around all week yelling insults while I picked up the rubbish. / Then I would be forced to stuff some dirty, sticky iceblock wrappers down her T-shirt ... and then I would get two weeks of picking up papers ... / 'Sorry,' I muttered, looking at the floor.

3. In this extract from *Indonesia* by Lisa Hill, highlight two places where new paragraphs should start.

Indonesian people have a strong sense of their own regional or tribal identity. / They describe themselves first as Bataks, Balinese, Sudanese, Irianese, Minangkabau and so on. / However, Javanese culture is dominant because the Javanese also led the struggle for independence and because the central government is on Java. / The first leader of independent Indonesia was President Sukarno. / He understood the importance of using symbols to develop unity amongst his different peoples. / He chose the mythical bird, Garuda, for the state crest. / Garuda was the powerful sun bird ridden by Prince Vishnu in Hindu mythology, and it was the symbol of the powerful old Javanese kingdom of Majapahit. / Although the Hindu religion has now mostly been replaced by Islam throughout Indonesia, Hindu stories and dance are still a very important part of Indonesian culture. / Garuda is also the name of the Indonesian international airline.

4. In this extract from *Do They Play Marbles On Mars?* by Margaret McAlister, highlight three places where new paragraphs should start.

'I saw that, Michael!' said Mrs Jackson. Come out here!' / 'What?' I tried to look innocent. 'What did I do?' / Mrs Jackson sighed. / She looked up at the ceiling then back at me. / 'Apologise to Cheryl.' / Now, that was really heavy. / It was only a bit of screwed-up paper. / Nobody ever died from being hit on the head by an old maths test.

Relevant and Irrelevant Information — Introduction

First we must understand what is meant by the words **relevant** and **irrelevant**.

If something is **relevant** you could also say it is appropriate or of some importance. It has some significance. If it is **irrelevant** then it is the opposite. It is inappropriate, unimportant or insignificant. When writing, only include material relevant to the topic.

It is important to understand the relevance of information when doing research at school. It is important to know what is more relevant or less relevant when we make plans to undertake certain tasks or activities. When we write fiction (creative writing) it is important to recognise whether the information is relevant, or not, to our story.

Can you find the irrelevant piece of information in this extract about weather?

Facts about weather.

- The temperature in Brisbane often reaches 25°C.
- Warm northerly winds increase the danger of bushfires.
- Bush walking in national parks is a popular pastime.
- Snow often falls on the southern ski slopes.
- Last spring, hail stones damaged many gardens.
- The dry, cool air was perfect for ripening grapes.

Q. Which point has the least to do with the weather?
A. Bush walking in national parks is a popular pastime.
Bush walking may be a pleasure any time of the year, summer, autumn, winter or spring. Some people may even enjoy doing it in the rain or snow!

Read *Indonesia* by Lisa Hill

The loudest explosion ever heard — when Krakatoa blew up!

Indonesia straddles one of the most unstable parts of the earth. There are many active volcanoes and earthquakes are common, so it is an interesting area for scientists to study fossil and geological activity.

Javanese and Sumatran children found it hard to concentrate on school work on the afternoon of 26 August, 1883. In the straits between Java and Sumatra, 160 kilometres away, the little volcanic island of Krakatoa had been rumbling away for months. Until now, no one had taken much notice because the volcano had rumbled and puffed before, but now the grumbling was interrupted by sharp sounds like thunderclaps that echoed all over the islands.

Terrified by the loud bangs, children rushed home to safety, but the noise was everywhere. No one slept much that night.

Just before seven o'clock the next morning, two immense explosions shook the ground beneath their feet. Doors blew open, and walls cracked. Whole buildings shook. There was an enormous volcanic eruption in which 35 000 people were killed. The island of Krakatoa had ceased to exist.

1. If you had to get information about the explosion on Krakatoa, which of the following facts would be most **irrelevant**? (tick as many boxes as you need)

- ☐ Indonesia is an interesting place for scientists to study fossils.
- ☐ Krakatoa is a volcanic island in the straits between Java and Sumatra.
- ☐ In August 1883 there were two explosions on Krakatoa.
- ☐ Before the explosions Krakatoa had been rumbling for months.

2. Select the most **relevant** information to complete this sentence. (circle one answer)
When Krakatoa blew up it (blew open doors   destroyed an island   made a noise).

Answers 1. Indonesia is an interesting place for scientists to study fossils. 2. destroyed an island

Relevant and Irrelevant Information — Night of the Muttonbirds

by Mary Small

Stopping in his tracks, he turned and looked back at this home; tin-roofed, weatherboard, ordinary, squatting comfortably in the hollow close to the creek. Smoke rose from the chimney. The sight brought tears to Matthew's eyes. It was all too familiar, too dear.

He put his fingers to his mouth and whistled. Kelpie came running, bounding ahead, game for another walk. Matthew felt honoured that he should give up the prospect of breakfast for him. He followed him down through the trees to the bay.

Kelpie scrabbled briskly in the sand, then rushed off to chase dotterels at the water's edge.

Matthew squatted down beside the boat to watch him.

He and Shelley had found the *Titch* at Christmas, washed up, abandoned on a beach on the other side of the island. Although both of the oars were missing, the boat was in good order and when it was brought back by truck to The Corner, nobody owned it. Matthew and Shelley and some of their friends made full use of it for fishing and diving. Now, with Matthew going it would hardly be used.

Opposite, across the glistening waters of Franklin Sound, the crumpled hills of the Strzeleckis on Flinders Island rose majestically into the blueness of the summer sky. To Matthew, it was very beautiful. For a long time he sat by the boat lost in his own thoughts. Then, whistling to Kelpie, he strode out along the length of the beach towards the narrow spit at the far end, scuffing his feet so hard in the sand that the soft, fine particles squeaked. A little way off, a group of terns and oystercatchers stood preening themselves.

1. Certain information is relevant if we have to understand the type of person Matthew is. Tick the boxes that are relevant to understanding Matthew's character.

- ☐ The view of the mountains impressed Matthew.
- ☐ Looking back at the house brought tears to Matthew's eyes.
- ☐ Matthew's dog, Kelpie, scrabbled briskly in the sand.
- ☐ The sand squeaked as Matthew walked along the beach.

2. Which words would be **irrelevant** when applied to Matthew? (tick as many boxes you need)

☐ watchful ☐ thoughtful ☐ friendly ☐ irate ☐ cruel ☐ content

3. What words would be **relevant** when applied to Flinders Island? (tick as many boxes you need)

☐ deserted ☐ busy ☐ hot ☐ cloudy ☐ natural ☐ barren

4. From the extract, what is the most important event about to affect Matthew's life?

____

5. According to the extract who is Matthew's regular companion? (tick one box)

☐ Titch ☐ Shelley ☐ Kelpie ☐ the fishermen

Relevant and Irrelevant Information — Desert Gold
The Search for Lasseter's Reef

by Mark Butler

The plan was for the expedition to head north from Alice Springs, then turn west towards Anna Downs station (now called Hamilton Downs), where they would fill their water tanks. Blakeley also intended to hire an Aboriginal guide there. The guide's job would be to make contact with any Aborigines they met and ask them about waterholes and about the country ahead of them.

If Lasseter was taking them on a wild-goose chase, then Blakeley wanted to make sure that everyone returned from it safely. With three vehicles and seven men travelling during a bad drought, he had to be sure that they could always find enough water. He knew that the best way to do that was to learn from the Aborigines.

After Anna Downs station, the expedition would head further west, to Illpilli Springs, a distance of 320 kilometres. Blakeley and Lasseter had agreed that Illpilli would be a good base camp for the expedition because it had a permanent source of water, as well as an airstrip and some crude shelters. In Sydney, Lasseter had made it clear that he believed the reef could be easily found once they were set up at Illpilli.

Blakeley decided to leave the Golden Quest in Alice Springs for the time being. When they reached Illpilli, Colson would drive Coote back to Alice Springs and Coote would fly back to Illpilli. Blakeley also planned to clear another airstrip at Yayai Creek, about halfway between Alice Springs and Illpilli, so the Golden Quest could land and refuel safely.

On paper, it looked a good plan. But the desert could ruin any plan.

1. If you were asked to describe how good Lasseter's party was at organising a desert trip what information would be **relevant** in preparing your description? (tick two boxes)

☐ It was decided to use local Aborigines as guides.

☐ Anna Downs station has been renamed Hamilton Downs.

☐ At Illpilli there were some crude shelters.

☐ An airstrip was planned for Yayai Creek.

2. What words would be **irrelevant** when applied to Lasseter? (tick as many boxes as you need)

☐ wary ☐ spiteful ☐ daring ☐ disorganised ☐ timid ☐ adventurous

3. What words would be **relevant** when describing the desert? (tick as many boxes as you need)

☐ safe ☐ harsh ☐ without services ☐ mountainous ☐ difficult ☐ bare

4. According to the extract, what is the purpose of the expedition? ______________________

____

5. Blakeley was a person that Lasseter couldn't trust. ☐ True ☐ False

6. The *Golden Quest* is the name of Blakeley's vehicle. ☐ True ☐ False

7. Lasseter believes that the reef would be easily found once at Illpilli. ☐ True ☐ False

8. Coote would fly the *Golden Quest* from Alice Springs to Illpilli. ☐ True ☐ False

Relevant and Irrelevant Information — Technology For The Environment

by Mike Callaghan & Peter Knapp

Soil erosion

Soil erosion is the natural process where soil is carried away by water and wind and deposited somewhere else, usually at the bottom of the ocean. Usually, the process of erosion is balanced by the processes which build the soil up. Scientists estimate that the natural process of soil formation can take from 100 to 2500 years to produce about 2.5cm of top soil, which contains the nutrients necessary for plant growth.

Plants and trees hold the topsoil in place. When plants and trees are removed, the topsoil is exposed and is easily washed away by rain, or blown away by the wind. The wrong use of technology and poor land management can destroy soil that took millions of years to develop, in just ten years.

The natural process of erosion has increased since humans began to plough the soil for crops and clear the land to feed large numbers of grazing animals. Bad land management practices, such as ploughing and clearing steep slopes, using too much irrigation and having too many animals grazing on pastures, all help to remove vegetation and leave the soil open to the effects of wind and rain. Perhaps the most destructive practice is the removal of forest. At present, we remove 12 million hectares of forest each year. Because of all of these practices, the world loses approximately 75 billion tonnes of soil each year. At this rate, we will lose 18 per cent of the farmable land on earth by the year 2000.

1. What information is **relevant** to understanding that soil erosion is a result of human activity? (tick as many boxes as you need)

- ☐ ploughing the land
- ☐ the topsoil is held in place by trees
- ☐ soil formation takes over 100 years
- ☐ increased numbers of grazing animals

2. All bad land management practices eventually cause soil erosion because ____________

____.

3. The formation of 2.5 cm of new soil (circle one letter)

(A) will happen by the year 2000.
(B) could take over a thousand years.
(C) takes millions of years.
(D) can happen in just ten years.

4. What words are **relevant** to erosion caused by people? (tick as many boxes as you need)

- ☐ irrigation
- ☐ hillsides
- ☐ nutrients
- ☐ pastures
- ☐ crops
- ☐ clearing

5. You have to get information on **natural soil erosion**. What facts are relevant?

(A) 18% of farmland will be lost by the year 2000.
(B) Soil erosion is balanced by soil build up.
(C) Wind and rain erosion increases when trees are removed.
(D) Much soil ends up at the bottom of the ocean.

6. Soil erosion was taking place before people began working the soil. ☐ True ☐ False

Fact and Opinion — Introduction

Facts and opinions are part of our everyday speech and writing. It is important to know when someone is trying to persuade you to do or believe something (See Understanding Persuasion p. 47).

A fact is something that everyone agrees with and can usually be proved either by direct observation or clear written records.

An opinion is a particular viewpoint of the writer or speaker.

An opinion often:

- is personal,
- is used to influence (or convince) the reader or listener,
- provides suggestions on courses of action (what to do).

Read this extract from *Technology for the environment* by M. Callaghan and P. Knapp.

> Oil is the most used energy fuel in the world. In America, the world's biggest consumer, oil makes up about 40 percent of its energy needs. Oil is also being used up faster and faster, and future supplies will become more difficult and expensive to mine.

Fact: *Oil is the most used energy fuel in the world.* This could be proved by doing some research, and comparing its use with other fuels (coal, gas, steam).

Opinion: Future supplies will become more difficult and expensive to mine. This may be so but it cannot be proved. It is quite possible new cheap ways of obtaining crude oil may be discovered.

Fact: *In America, the world's biggest consumer, oil makes up about 40 percent of its energy needs.* It may be difficult to do but this fact could be checked.

Shaping the news

by John D. Fitzgerald

> Because the news is such an important program, each television station tries to make its news stand out from the rest. To a large extent the station does this by trying to create an **image** for its news that will make it widely recognised.
>
> An **image** has several parts. One is the logo the station designs. Another is the music it uses to begin and end the program. The purpose of the logo is to provide the viewer with a consistent image, and to remind them that they are about to watch the news on a particular channel. The music is also part of the image that separates the news from other programs. It is like a trumpet call to let viewers know the news is about to start. A third part which separates the news on one channel from that on another is the newsreader.

Write **fact** or **opinion** to describe the information taken from the extract. (Questions 1 to 4)

1. The news is such an important program. __________

2. Music is used to begin and end a news program. __________

3. The purpose of the logo is to provide the viewer with a consistent image. __________

4. Each television station tries to make its news stand out from the rest. __________

5. Most of the information in the extract is fact. ☐ True ☐ False

6. TV stations use two methods to make their news widely recognised. ☐ True ☐ False

Answers 1. opinion, 2. fact, 3. fact, 4. fact, 5. True, 6. False (3 methods are used)

Fact and Opinion — 2

Read the extracts on this page and answer the questions on **fact and opinion.**

The Thunder God

by David Shapiro

Many centuries ago in China, there lived along the Yellow River, in a small village, two boys named Fei and Yo. Fei was a fine student while Yo liked neither school nor study.

Now Fei and Yo, though different, were best of friends. Yo was never jealous of Fei's good marks but happy he had a friend who always did well in examinations. And Fei was full of admiration for the way that Yo could handle a hoe, scythe or sickle.

1. Tick the box that is an **opinion** which is taken from the extract.

- ☐ Many centuries ago two boys lived in China.
- ☐ Fei was a fine student.
- ☐ The Chinese boys' names were Fei and Yo.
- ☐ Fei and Yo, though different, were best of friends.

2. Though this extract is part of a folk tale most of the information is presented as facts.

☐ True ☐ False

Framing Ned Kelly

by Louise Martin-Chew

St Kilda was a lively place in the summer; crowded with holiday-makers. However, in the winter it was cold, bleak and eerily empty.

Sidney's father became a tram driver in Melbourne. He sometimes arranged for Sidney to travel on the trams for free. As a result, Sidney saw a lot of the city. Mr Nolan was also a keen member of the Tramways Lifesaving Club. Sidney used to accompany his father to the St Kilda Pool each Sunday during the summer.

Sidney's mother loved going to the cinema and much to the **dismay** of Sidney's school, would keep him home with her every Friday so that he could accompany her. This may have helped Sidney to develop an interest in the appearance of the shapes and colours he **observed** in objects and in nature.

After he left school, Sidney had a difficult time finding a job. This was the 1930s, in a period known as the Great Depression. Work was **scarce**, but Sidney was a likeable young man, and **managed** to get a number of jobs. Some of them he hated and worked at for only a short time.

3. Tick the box which is an **opinion** taken from the above extract.

- ☐ Days off school may have helped Sidney to develop an interest in painting.
- ☐ After he left school, Sidney had a difficult time finding a job.
- ☐ Sidney was kept home from school every Friday.
- ☐ Sidney's mother loved going to the cinema.

4. Which word warns the reader that the information is probably an opinion? (tick one box)

☐ dismay ☐ observed ☐ scarce ☐ managed

5. It is a **fact** that winter in Melbourne is bleak and eerie. ☐ True ☐ False

Fact and Opinion — Antarctica

by John Collerson

Antarctica is a uniquely beautiful part of the world whose fragile environment is a delicate balance of natural forces and living creatures. It is very little disturbed by human contact and almost completely free from pollution. There are different ideas about what we should do with Antarctica. Many scientists and other feel that, apart from scientific research, it should be left alone. If it is preserved we can learn a lot about the rest of the world from it. Bubbles of air tapped in the ice and the nature of the ice itself can tell scientists about the earth's atmosphere and climate at various times in the past and so changes in the earth's climate, pollution levels and the greenhouse effect are able to be seen. If Antarctica itself becomes polluted, the usefulness of this measure will be lost. Antarctica also plays an important part in the control of our weather and climate. Too much interference could upset these benefits. Other people say that we should open up Antarctica for tourism or use it as a source of food and mineral resources for the world's needs.

Since people have been going to the Antarctic the problem of pollution has arisen. Although there is little pollution in the continent as a whole, a few bases and expeditions have polluted some areas. In Antarctica rubbish does not decompose as it does in warmer climates and it is not possible to bury anything as the ice-free ground is mainly solid rock. So rubbish just accumulates or is blown about by the wind — even scrap metal. There have also been oil spills and dumping of rubbish at sea by ships. Today there is better control and some rubbish has to be taken back to the home country. Another set of problems comes with the transport needs of the bases, especially the building of airstrips, which can damage the environment greatly. These problems will be magnified if too many people continue to go to Antarctica. So we must face the question: what should we do with Antarctica?

1. Tick the box that is an opinion taken from the above extract.

☐ Since people have been going to the Antarctic, pollution has become a problem.

☐ Antarctica is a uniquely beautiful part of the world.

☐ There are different ideas about what we should do with Antarctica.

☐ In Antarctica rubbish does not decompose as it does in warmer climates.

Answer the next 4 questions with information according to the extract.

2. *An airstrip will greatly damage the Antarctic environment* is a **fact**. ☐ True ☐ False

3. The writer is expressing an **opinion** when he writes 'Problems will be magnified if too many people continue to go to Antarctica'. ☐ True ☐ False

4. The nature of the ice can tell scientists about the earth's atmosphere and climate at various times in the past. This is an opinion. ☐ True ☐ False

5. Generally, the writer's opinion is that there is still time to save Antarctica from environmental damage. ☐ True ☐ False

6. It is a fact that to get rid of rubbish in Antarctica it must be (tick one)

☐ buried in holes in the ice-free surface. ☐ taken back to the country it came from.

7. In your opinion should mining be allowed in Antarctica? (short answer) ______
Can you give a reason for your opinion? (no written answer required)

8. Where might you get other information to prove or disprove that pollution is a problem in Antarctica? ______________________________

Fact and Opinion — Eyes of the world

by David Bolliger

This extract is about the importance of photos in newspapers. Read p. 6 for more information on Bruce Miller as a photo journalist.

The story, **Safe from Sharks?**, began to take shape when a gentleman rang the newspaper to say that he had noticed that the shark net at Nielson Park had a lot of holes in it. He had heard that other shark nets around the harbour had holes in them and wanted to know if he was safe. So Bruce (Miller) got an underwater camera and went for a swim around the shark nets to have a look at them. He did not find a lot of holes!

(Bruce Miller then took an underwater photo of the legs of the gentleman who reported the holes as though a shark is looking at the legs through a hole in the net.)

The photo made it to the front page of the newspaper because it appeals to the readers sense of fear about sharks. People want to know whether they are safe, so they buy a paper to find out. There was probably much more important news to tell, but the editors knew that this photo would be a good selling point.

The headlines, together with the photo, give the impression that it is not safe to swim. But the council was very embarrassed about the newspaper covering the story. As soon as they heard that Bruce (Miller) was taking photos, they began to remove the nets altogether, because they did not have the funds to replace them! The council seemed more worried about bad press than the possibility of someone being hurt by a shark. From this fact you should be able to make up your own mind whether the headline is exaggerating the danger or not.

1. Tick the box that is an **opinion** taken from the above extract.
   - ☐ It had been reported that shark nets around the harbour had holes in them.
   - ☐ Bruce Miller's photo made it to the front page of the newspaper.
   - ☐ A man rang the paper to say that the shark net at Nielson Park had holes in it.
   - ☐ The council seemed more worried about bad press than someone being attacked.
2. 'People want to know whether they are safe, so they buy a paper to find out.' This information is an opinion. ☐ True ☐ False
3. The article **Safe from Sharks?** comes from a ______________ which should prepare the reader for writing that contains **facts** as well as ______________.
4. It is a **fact** that there was probably more important news in the paper than the article **Safe from Sharks?**. ☐ True ☐ False
5. Which of the following statements, from the extract, is an opinion? (circle one letter)
   (A) Miller's photo appealed to the reader's sense of fear.
   (B) The council was very embarrassed by the shark story.
   (C) Miller got an underwater camera and went for a swim around the shark nets.
   (D) Miller did not find a lot of holes in the shark nets.
6. It is a **fact** that you should be able to make up your mind if the article is exaggerating.
   ☐ True ☐ False
7. Which phrase from the extract prepares the reader for information that is probably an opinion? (tick one box)
   ☐ gives the impression ☐ wants to know ☐ when a gentleman rang

Understanding Persuasion — Introduction

Almost without being aware of it, we are bombarded with persuasion everyday. You cannot watch television, listen to the radio or read a magazine without advertisements. Advertisements are trying to get you to choose a particular **product** or **service**. In fact, you can't drive down the road without seeing advertisements.

But there are other ways people use persuasion. Your friends at school may try to persuade you to join them in a game. Another student may try to persuade you that he or she is the best person for class or school captain. These people are trying to persuade you to think in a particular way. They are trying to influence your **thinking**. **Persuasive writing** has some special features.

- it tries to attract the reader's attention,
- it may use a mixture of **logical** and **emotive** language,
- it sounds **convincing** (as if the writer is an expert!),
- it may contain a **slogan** and a **concluding statement**,
- it often appears to address the reader/listener in a personal way.

Read this ad from a suburban newspaper.

Put yourself in the spotlight!
Take centre stage

Our Motto: *We will put you on the road to* ***STARDOM!***

Debbie's Spotlight Drama School
Certificates for all who complete the three week course.
Also classes in: singing, miming, and dancing.

Learning Points

- speaks to the reader directly by using the words **yourself** and **you**
- attracts the reader's attention by a picture and big print for the heading
- this ad appeals to your **emotions** more than your common sense **(logic)**
- the ad gives the impression that this could be happening for you right now!
- makes use of a **slogan**
- 'you' see yourself becoming a great star
- the certificate is an extra incentive
- concluding statement (other classes available)

1. Who are you supposed to think of instead of the person on the stage? ________________

2. What is the slogan for the drama school? ______________________________

3. This ad appeals to your emotions. ☐ True ☐ False

4. In actual fact, will everyone become a star? Yes/No (circle one)

5. Debbie has provided proof that she is an experienced drama teacher. Yes/No (circle one)

Answers 1. yourself, 2. We will put you on the road to stardom! 3. False, 4. No, 5. No

Understanding Persuasion — Earth First

by David Bowden & Jenny Dibley

In the book **Earth First** the authors investigate how shoppers are 'persuaded' to buy particular products. Read this extract and answer the questions, remembering the things you have read about persuasion.

Why do we consume so much?
Companies have employed many people and spent millions of dollars on advertising; creating new ways to sell products. Some methods used to entice consumers are listed below.

Time saving devices
Disposal items have become popular in the past twenty years. They are products we use only once, or a few times then throw away. These disposal products include drink and food containers, razors, tissues, pens and cameras. Disposal products are convenient for busy families. They have been designed to save time for our 'fast moving society'.

Extra, extra
It is common practice to produce items that require accessories that make them 'seem' complete. For example, a doll may have accessories such as clothing or a 'car' which are sold separately. Accessories cost more money and advertisements for them are designed to make us feel that our original purchase is incomplete without all its accessories.

Using famous faces
Famous people are often used by companies to **sell** their product. These people are usually actors, singers or sporting people. We are encouraged by them to buy items such as toys, hats, T-shirts, rulers, masks, posters, compact disks and videos. What happens to these products when the star is no longer popular?

Note: Before answering the questions it may help to re-read the information on p. 47.

1. According to the authors of **Earth First** advertising is often used to ________________

____.

2. The writers of the extract are trying to persuade you to look at how you react to advertising. To do this they have (circle one letter)
(A) used slogans.
(B) made use of highly emotional language.
(C) tried to convince the reader by using facts and figures.
(D) assumed the reader is an intelligent person.

3. The word **sell** is used in a special way. In the extract it means to (tick one box)

☐ take money for products. ☐ guarantee the quality.
☐ persuade people to buy. ☐ show the popularity.

4. Name a 'doll' that requires the owner to buy extra accessories? ____________

5. This extract is written to make the reader feel that (tick one box)

☐ he/she can now understand how advertising is used.
☐ there is too much advertising on TV.
☐ film stars should not be used to promote products they don't use.
☐ advertising is the best way of finding out what is for sale.

Understanding Persuasion — Desert Gold

by Mark Butler

Read this extract which includes a short speech given by Harold Lasseter. (On reading the extract you will find that it was actually made up by the author.)

The search for Lasseter's Reef

Imagine a small, stocky man addressing a crowd in a shady corner of Sydney's Hyde Park on a humid day in March 1930. He is talking about riches beyond anyone's wildest dreams — his slow, musical voice carries across the park, drawing more and more listeners towards him. As he speaks, he hands out pamphlets to as many members of his swelling audience as he can reach. Soon the audience is eagerly handing the pamphlets around for him.

'I tell you, this continent has a heart of solid gold! I've seen it, touched it! Gold is the basis of all wealth, and the gold I have seen will turn Australia into a wealthy country again. No more Depression — a job for every man, and debt banished forever. Think about it, read the pamphlet, then join with me. My friends, for a small investment you can save the country from ruin and become rich!'

Within minutes of finishing his speech, the man is surrounded by people, all of them offering him money ...

This scene is made up, but something like this happened in Sydney in 1930, when Harold Lasseter began telling his amazing story. He told of a 23 kilometre reef of gold he had found in unexplored desert country in central Australia — 'Lasseter's Reef', the richest goldmine in Australia!

1. In his speech, (paragraph 2) Lasseter uses some words and phrases that appeal to the listener's emotions. Other information adds to the reader's understanding. Tick the box for the statement that contains the LEAST **emotive** language.

- ☐ This continent has a heart of gold.
- ☐ Gold is the basis of all wealth.
- ☐ For a small investment you can save this country from ruin.
- ☐ Debt will be banished forever.

2. Lasseter's 'speech' is presented in such a way that the listeners believe (circle two letters)

(A) they have a chance to be wealthy.
(B) only a selected few can join in.
(C) that Lasseter wants each person to be part of his plans.
(D) the project will be very risky.

3. This speech is meant to make the audience feel (tick one box)

☐ angry. ☐ excited. ☐ hopeless. ☐ informed.

4. Which idea from the speech is repeated several times? (tick one box)

- ☐ riches are readily available
- ☐ the gold was easy to mine
- ☐ the Depression causes hardship
- ☐ people out of work should have work

5. Lasseter provided the audience with facts and figures which convinced them he was telling the truth. ☐ True ☐ False

6. People in the audience were paid to hand out pamphlets. ☐ True ☐ False

Understanding Persuasion — Earth First

by David Bowden & Jenny Dibley

Note: This extract comes just after the information on p. 48 (Understanding Persuasion).

Why do we consume so much?

Sale time

Bargain sales are a great way to tempt consumers. Most shops have sales regularly, to move old or discontinued stock. Are there really bargains in these shops or is it just a way to get you to buy the products even if you don't need them?

A lot of money is spent on advertising bargains. How often have you run to the letterbox, seeing there is something in it, possibly a letter for you, only to find a wad of advertising material?

Most forms of advertising follow a simple format. Advertisements promote a way of life that is presented as ideal. People in advertisements are usually attractive, happy, own expensive cars and houses and generally promote a high standard of living. Is this really how most people live?

'Hurry before they all run out!'

There are many ways of persuading us to consume. Sometimes we shop to the sound of a voice telling us we can get 'two for the price of one!' or 'hurry before they all run out'. We are often told that 'an offer like this will never be repeated'. The implication is that we cannot live without these products.

1. The writers have included questions in the extract. These questions are meant to

(A) be answered by the reader. (C) be given to shopkeepers to answer.
(B) make the reader think about the subject. (D) help readers with their research.

2. The main reason for salespeople saying 'hurry before they all run out' is to (tick one box)

☐ make sure all buyers have a chance to buy.
☐ inform consumers that the amount of stock is in short supply.
☐ persuade the buyer that there is a need to purchase the item quickly.
☐ sell stock that is very popular.

3. Advertisers have many ways of persuading consumers to buy. ☐ True ☐ False

4. Most advertising uses ordinary people in ordinary situations. ☐ True ☐ False

5. Has anyone in your family bought something they didn't really want? ______________

What was it and why did they do it? ______________________________

6. The writers of this extract use a writing technique often used by advertisers. It is (tick one box)

☐ speaking to the reader in a very personal, friendly manner.
☐ making the matter so urgent that the reader must act immediately.
☐ repeating the same information and slogans over and over again.
☐ appealing to the reader's need to be part of a better way of life.

7. This extract is meant to (tick one box)

☐ make you more suspicious of advertising. ☐ convince you that advertising is for your benefit.

Understanding and Using a Table of Contents

Most factual books have a table of contents. These are found in the front of the book, usually within the first few pages. A table of contents is a quick reference which helps readers find the main sections of the book. Some books are broken up into major sections, subjects or topics and within each section or subject area there are sub-sections.

Books of fiction may also have a table of contents. These give the chapter pages or, if a book of many works, the page on which individual stories, plays or poems are located.

Here is a contents table from **Australia's Inland Sea** by Dr T. Flannery and P. Kendall.

Contents

1 The myth of an inland sea 6
Where did the rivers flow? 6
Sturt explores the interior 9
Evidence for an inland sea 11
2 Australia at the time of the inland sea 14
The Cretaceous Period 14
A living landscape 18
3 How and why did the inland sea form? 26
Advancing waters 27
4 Animals of the inland sea 29
Invertebrates 29
Vertebrates 34
Plesiosaurs 37
Pliosaurs 39
Ichthyosaurs 41
A flying reptile 43
5 Plants and animals of the inland sea 47
The first flowering plants 51
Fish and insects 51
Dinosaurs 54
6 The inland sea today 58
Suggested reading for more information 60
Glossary 62
Index 64

Page numbers are often in columns. In this book they are at the end of each line.

Main headings/Chapters (in bold)

Sub-headings (in plain font)

Suggested reading includes other books on the same topic.

The **glossary** is an explanation of unusual words or phrases used in the book. It is in dictionary order.

The **index** is an alphabetical list of the many topics covered in the book with their page numbers (see p. 53).

Note: some contents tables include a bibliography.
A **bibliography** is a list of other books referred to in the text.

1. On what page would you find information about dinosaurs? page __________

2. What is the main heading for 'A flying reptile'? ______________________________

3. The section, **The inland sea today**, begins on page 58. ☐ True ☐ False

4. The section, **The myth of an inland sea**, is the longest section. ☐ True ☐ False

5. To find out about Sturt, the explorer, you would turn to page 9. ☐ True ☐ False

6. The word **cycads** is used in the book. Where would I first look to find all references to **cycads** in the book? In the ________________.

Answers 1. page 54, 2. Animals of the inland sea, 3. True, 4. False, 5. True, 6. Index

Understanding and Using a Table of Contents — Homeland Australia

by Michael Dugan

Contents

Introduction	1
Australia Needs People	2
Life in a new land	7
The people who came	7
An end to the White Australia Policy	13
Another wave of refugees	13
Problems of settlement	16
Migrant hostels	23
Assimilation	25
Work	27
Language	31
Good Neighbour movement	35
Changes	37
An end to assimilation	37
The migrants organise	42
Ethnic broadcasting	46
Multicultural Australia	48
Glossary	54
Bibliography	55
Index	57

1. On what page will you find the index? page ________

2. On what page will you find out about Ethnic broadcasting? page ________

3. What is the last topic in the book? ________________________

4. **Japan** is referred to in the book. Where would I first look to find all references to Japan? In the ____________.

5. To find the meaning of the word **refugees** you would use the Index. ☐ True ☐ False

6. There are two topics on page 13. ☐ True ☐ False

7. How many sub-headings are included under **Life in a new land**? ______________

8. What is the section called that starts on page 54? ______________________

9. The Introduction is found at the ________ of the book. The Index is at the ______.

10. Where in the book would you find the **Contents page**? In the ______________.

Understanding and Using an Index — Introduction

Many factual books have indexes. They are found in the back of the book. Indexes are a quick reference which help readers find the information in a book that is not easily found using the Table of Contents. The index items are listed **alphabetically** and give one, or more pages, where information may be found. References longer than one page are shown by using a hyphen (eg 34–37).

One of the main skills in using an index is finding the right reference word. If you wanted to find some information on ***motor cars*** you might have to look under ***cars***. If you wanted to find information on ***rainfall*** you might have to look under ***weather***. If you don't find what you are looking for the first time try some other possibilities.

Indexes may also have their own short cuts. The main entry may not be repeated to save space (a bit like a dictionary). If you wanted to find **diets** you may have to look up **human health**. Other information on human health may also be listed, eg **allergies**.

Read the index from **Earth First** by D. Bowden & J. Dibley and answer the questions.

Index (incomplete)

Aborigines 5
advertising 12, 18, 25, 27–28, 29, 30
Africa 12
America 12
animals 11, 23, 31
  animal testing 2, 35
Asia 12
Australia 2, 3, 4, 5, 7, 8, 13, 14, 17, 20, 22, 23, 24
Britain 5
calcium silicate 37
chemicals
  harmful/toxic 2, 8, 15, 17, 18, 37
chlorofluorocarbons (CFSs) 8, 14, 15, 23–24, 30, 37
compost 11
consumer affairs 8
consumption 2, 4, 9, 11
Container Deposit Legislation, South Australia 13-14
developing nations 4, 8, 10,12
developed countries 4, 8, 9, 10, 11, 12
economic growth 9
  needs 4
  wants 4
electricity 11, 20, 22, 32
  hydro-electricity 22
energy 2, 10, 11, 32–33
  energy-efficient products 32, 33
  energy-rating labels 8, 32
environmental consumerism 10
Europe 5
fast-food see takeaway food
fluorocarbons 24
garbage see waste
glass 33
greenhouse effect 13
greenhouse gases 14, 22
household waste see waste
human health 13, 15, 22, 32, 35
  allergies 36
  food additives 36-37
  respiratory problems 22
  diets 7
  cooking habits 7
  natural ingredients 35, 36
industrialisation 5
  technology 7
insects 18, 23, 35, 36
  insect sprays 18, 23, 35
living standards 4, 9, 10, 28
local councils 14
mannitol 37
markets 10-11
mass production 7
mercury 17
monosodium glutamate (MSG) 36
non-renewable resources see resources
ozone layer 13, 23, 37
packaging 6, 11, 22, 35, 38
  excessive 2, 15, 22, 23, 26, 32
paper 20, 22, 23, 26, 33, 34, 35
  recycled 33
PET bottles see products

1. On what page would you find information on glass? page ___________

2. How many references are there to ***ozone layer*** in the index? ___________

3. If you wanted to find out about **recycled paper** you would look under ___________.

4. There are two different entries for **Markets** listed. ☐ True ☐ False

5. To find **fast foods** you will have to look under **takeaway food**. ☐ True ☐ False

6. The most information on **energy** commences on page (2 10 11 32). (circle one answer)

Answers 1. p. 33, 2. three, 3. paper, 4. False, 5. True, 6. p. 32 (and onto p. 33)

Understanding and Using an Index — Shaping the News

by John D. Fitzgerald

Numbers in bold refer to illustrations.

Index (incomplete)

ABC radio, 34
  news, 6
ABC TV, 18
  news, 27
accuracy of media, 39
Age, the, 6
America's Cup, 7
Ash Wednesday 1983, 29-30
Ashes, the, 7

Berlin Wall, **8**
BHP, 35

Cave, Peter, **29**
Channel Nine, **19**, 26-27
Channel Ten Eyewitness News, 27
conflict, 3, 39
Cottee, Kay, 7
court cases, **20**
crime, 4
current affairs, 33

D-cart technology, **35**
Delahunty, Mary, **21**, 27

Gulf war, 29

Henderson, Brian, **26**-27
Herald-Sun, News-Pictorial, 11
human interest, 6

Johnston, David, 27

Koori viewpoints, **14**
Kostakidis, Mary, **17**, 22
Koval, Ramona, 33-34

logging of forests, **33**

media sources, 40
Morecroft, Richard, 23
Murphy, Paul, **17**
Murray, Les, **17**

Newcastle, NSW, 5, 14
newspapers, 2-14
  timing of news, 40
newsworthiness, 3-8, 39-40
  variations on, 8
Nicoll, Murray, 30
Nyngan, NSW, 5, 14

oddities, 6
outstanding feats, 6-7

photographs, newspaper, 13-15
pictures, 24-25
  television, 17-18

radio, 28-38
  first with news, 40
  form of the news, 34-37
  image of the news, 38
  transitions in, 35
Rainbow Warrior, **8**, 36, 37

SBS television, 17-18, **26**
Scott, James, 7

1. On what page would you find **information** about **Nyngan** (NSW)? page ____________

2. If I looked up **Channel Nine** and went to page 19 what would I find? ____________

3. The reference on **radio** commences on page 28 and finishes on page ____________.

4. To what word do you go, to find information on Paul Murphy? ____________

5. The entry **photographs** comes before **pictures**. ☐ True ☐ False

6. The photograph of the **Rainbow Warrior** is on page 36. ☐ True ☐ False

7. This index, **Shaping the news**, is arranged in alphabetical order. ☐ True ☐ False

8. To find the entry on **the Ashes** you have to look under **Ashes, the**. Explain why?

____

9. There are (2 3 4) references in the index to **newsworthiness**. (circle one number)

Using Timetables — Introduction

Timetables play an important part in our lives. Some of us use timetables for bus or train travel. We have lesson timetables at school but we also have timetables for sports days. The program for the school concert is a type of timetable.

Timetables are a list of events according to time — when things are on. Without timetables we could be late for school. Timetables help us to keep our lives in order.

Bus and ferry timetables require the careful reading of tables. You may have to read across the table as well us up and down the table. This is a timetable for a tour operator who has **one ferry** and **one bus** that travel between Devonport and Auckland.

Devonport — Auckland
Tourist Bus and Ferry Holiday Timetable

Tour Ferry departs from: Devonport		Tour Ferry departs from: Auckland		Tour Bus departs from: Devonport	Tour Bus departs from: Auckland
AM	6.30	AM	7.00	AM 6.45	7.45
	7.30		8.00	8.45	9.45
	8.30		9.00	10.45	11.45
	9.30		10.00		
	10.30		11.00		
PM	12.30	PM	1.00	PM 12.45	1.45
	2.30		3.00	2.45	3.45
	3.30		4.00	4.45	5.45
	4.30		5.00		
	5.30		6.00		

Give **short answers** for questions 1 to 5.

1. The Tour Ferry departs Devonport every hour commencing at ____________ .

2. The first Tour Bus departs Devonport at ____________ .

3. This is a special timetable for ____________ .

4. How many Tour Ferry departures from Auckland are there each day? ____________

5. The last ferry trip for the day departs from ____________ at ____________ .

6. There are more bus tours between the two points than ferry tours. ☐ True ☐ False

7. The trip from Auckland to Devonport is quicker by bus. ☐ True ☐ False

8. The bus trip between Auckland and Devonport takes about an hour. ☐ True ☐ False

9. How many afternoon bus trips from Auckland to Devonport are there? ____________

Answers 1. 6:30 am, 2. 6:45 am, 3. holidays, 4. ten, 5. Auckland at, 6 pm, 6. False, 7. False, 8. True, 9. 3

Using Timetables — TV guide

A TV guide is a list of programs arranged according to when they are screened. Use the Pacific Post TV guide to answer the questions below.

SATURDAY Jan 22 **Pacific Post** TV guide

ABN		NTV		SBV	
Noon	Sports World: (includes reports from today's tennis, golf, bowls and horse racing)	**Noon**	Midday Movie: Class of '95 **G**	**Noon**	Stage divers
				1.00	Report from Britain **Rpt**
		2.00	State Athletics: Championships		
				2.30	Sky Devils G
3.00	News update			**3.00**	Top Golf Courses
3.15	Sports World				
		4.00	Lost in Space **Rpt**	**4.00**	Theatre News
5.00	News and weather			**5.00**	Pet hotline
5.30	What's cooking?	**5.30**	News and weather	**5.30**	Cartoon break
		6.00	Sports review	**6.00**	News and weather
6.30	Wildlife Park	**6.30**	Holiday Line	**6.30**	Just Stop It! **G**
7.30	Police Squad **Rpt**	**7.30**	Our Street **G**	**7.30**	Explorer Lost **G**
8.30	Art report **M**	**8.30**	Night Train **PG**	**8.30**	Movie: Ozone **PG**

Programs G — General PG — Parent guidance M — Mature audience
R — Adult Rpt — Repeat S — Sub-titles

Give **short answers** for questions 1 to 6.

1. Which channel has News at 3 pm? _____
2. How long is **Our Street** on NTV? _____
3. Is **Art report** suitable for children? _____
4. Which channel has the most sport? _____
5. What does **Rpt** stand for? _____________
6. When do 'adult type' shows begin? ____
7. Name a program that requires parent guidance. ________________________.
8. If I watched **Police Squad** I would miss **Night Train**. ☐ True ☐ False
9. The first full evening news report is on at 5.30. ☐ True ☐ False
10. The **Sports World** program is interrupted by a **News update**. ☐ True ☐ False
11. What program might I watch to find out about caring for pets? __________________
12. This program was published in a paper. Which paper? __________________
13. What day is this program for? __________________
14. What show follows the NTV **Sports review**? __________________
15. Use the numbers 1, 2, 3, and 4 to show the order in which these shows are screened.

☐ Wildlife Park ☐ Sky Devils ☐ Our Street ☐ Lost in Space

Understanding Maps — Introduction

We usually think of an **atlas** when we think of maps. But maps can be found in many other places. Most people who live in big cities use a **street directory**. People who do a lot of travelling might use a **road map**. People interested in the universe might use a **star map**. When studying maps we are usually interested in distance and direction.

This map comes from **Indonesia** by Lisa Hill (p. 24).

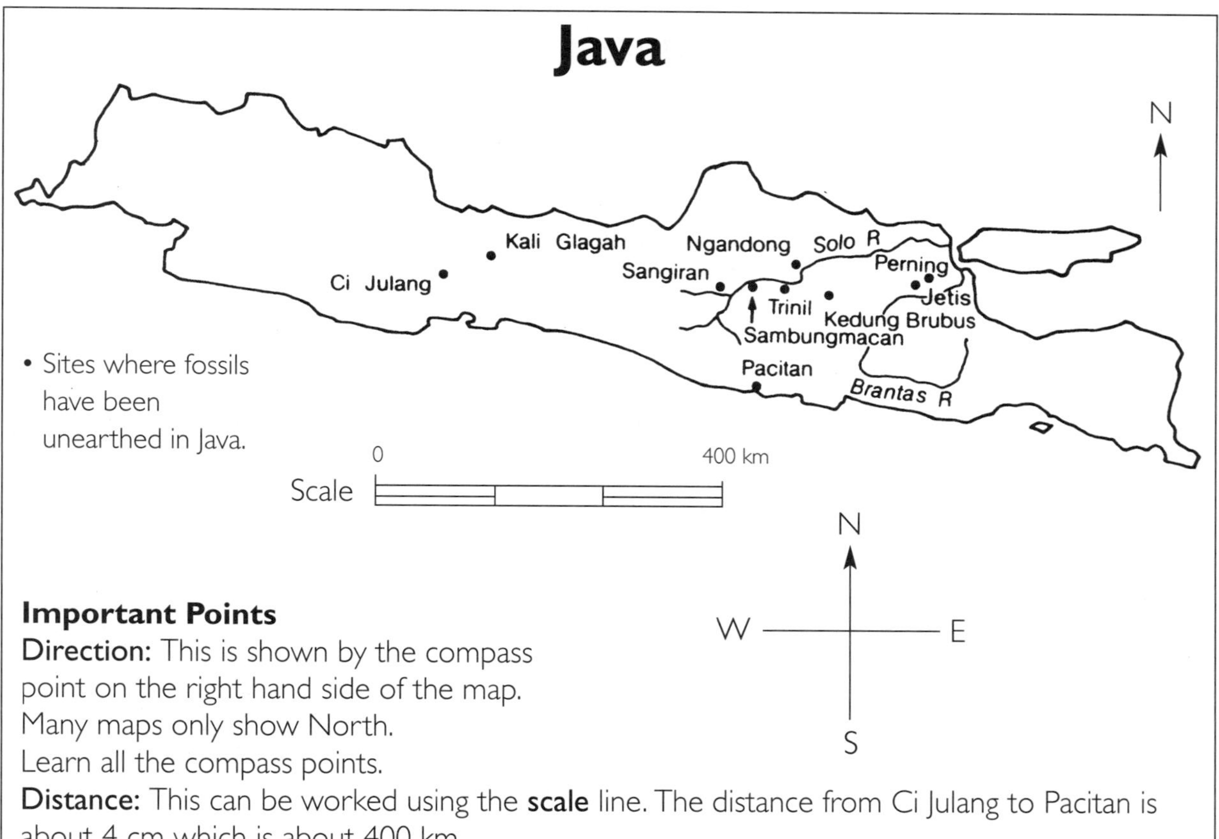

Important Points

Direction: This is shown by the compass point on the right hand side of the map. Many maps only show North. Learn all the compass points.

Distance: This can be worked using the **scale** line. The distance from Ci Julang to Pacitan is about 4 cm which is about 400 km.

Key: Information (usually in symbol form) that helps you interpret the map. The • is a quick reference to all fossil sites.

Give **short answers** for questions 1 to 6.

If you were in **Sangiran**, which direction would you go to get to

1. Ci Julang? _________ **2.** Pacitan? _________ **3.** Perning? _________

4. About how far from Kali Glagah to Ngandong? about_________ km

5. Name one river in Java. ____________________

6. In how many places have fossils been found in Java? _________

7. The town furthest to the west is (Ci Julang Jetis Perning). (circle one)

8. The most southerly town is (Trini Kedung Brubus Pacitan). (circle one)

Answers 1. west, 2. south, 3. east, 4. 300 km, 5. Solo OR Brantas, 6. ten, 7. Ci Julang, 8. Pacitan

Understanding Maps — The islands of Manihiki (Cook Islands)

Note: Some maps use **coordinates**. Coordinates make it easy to give locations.
The coordinates for Motu Poia are K5.

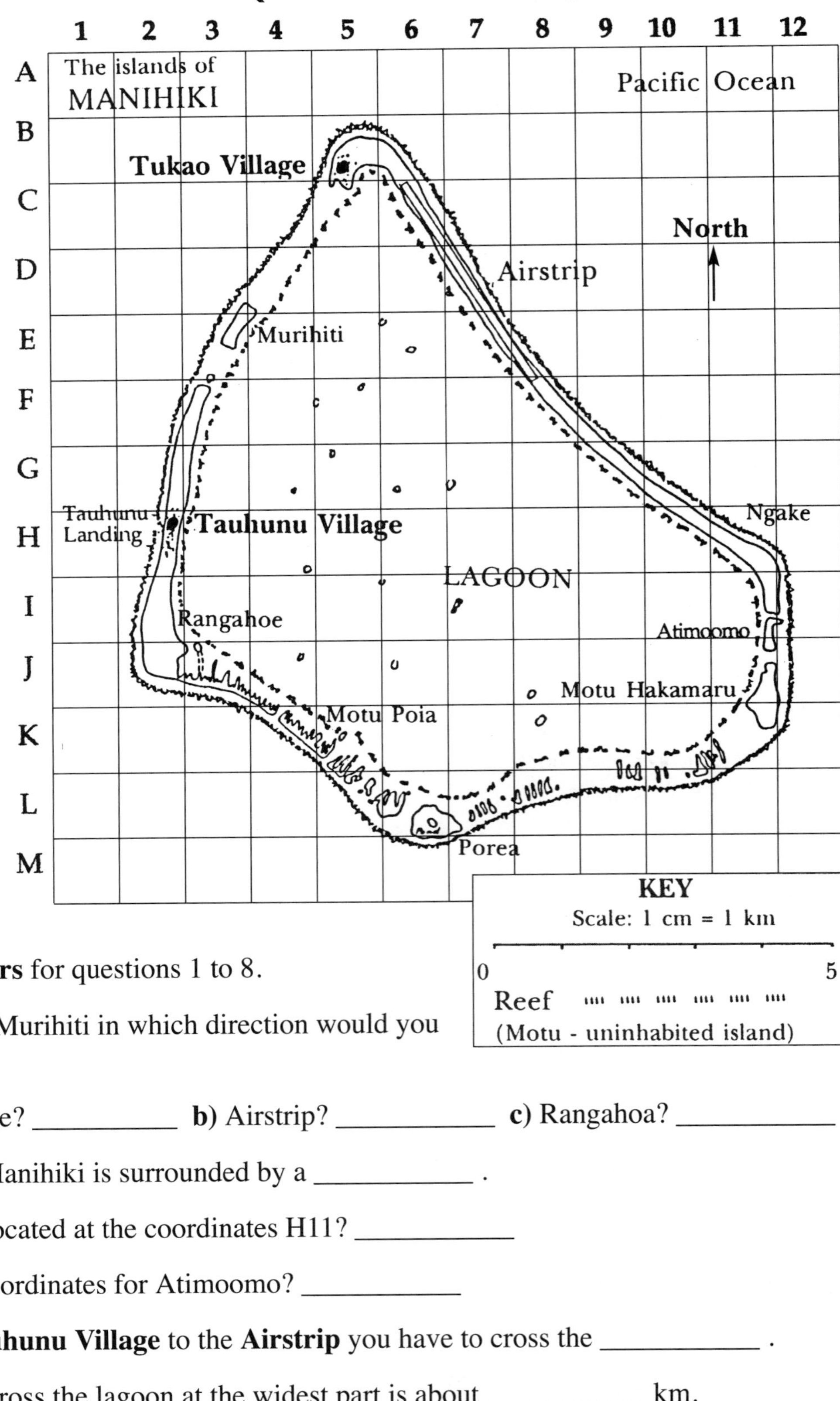

Give **short answers** for questions 1 to 8.

1. If you were on Murihiti in which direction would you go to get to

a) Tukao Village? __________ **b)** Airstrip? __________ **c)** Rangahoa? __________

2. The whole of Manihiki is surrounded by a __________ .

3. What place is located at the coordinates H11? __________

4. What are the coordinates for Atimoomo? __________

5. To go from **Tauhunu Village** to the **Airstrip** you have to cross the __________ .

6. The distance across the lagoon at the widest part is about __________ km.

7. Manihiki is made up of many small islands. ☐ True ☐ False

Understanding Graphs and Charts — Introduction

Graphs and charts provide information that has to be read in a particular way. Charts, graphs and tables (see p. 55) require you to understand how the information is presented, as well as interpreting the information provided.

Charts and graphs are a simple way of providing information without a lot of reading.

In maths you may have learned that graphs come in many forms. These include pictographs, bar or column graphs, line graphs and pie graphs. Information in many books is often provided in graph form because it can save lengthy explanations. Most graphs show the relationship between two pieces of information.

These **graphs** are **pie graphs**. They give information about how well land is being cared for in each state and territory. It is from **Technology For The Environment** (p. 34) by Mike Callaghan and Peter Knapp. (Note: **degraded** land is land that has been poorly cared for.)

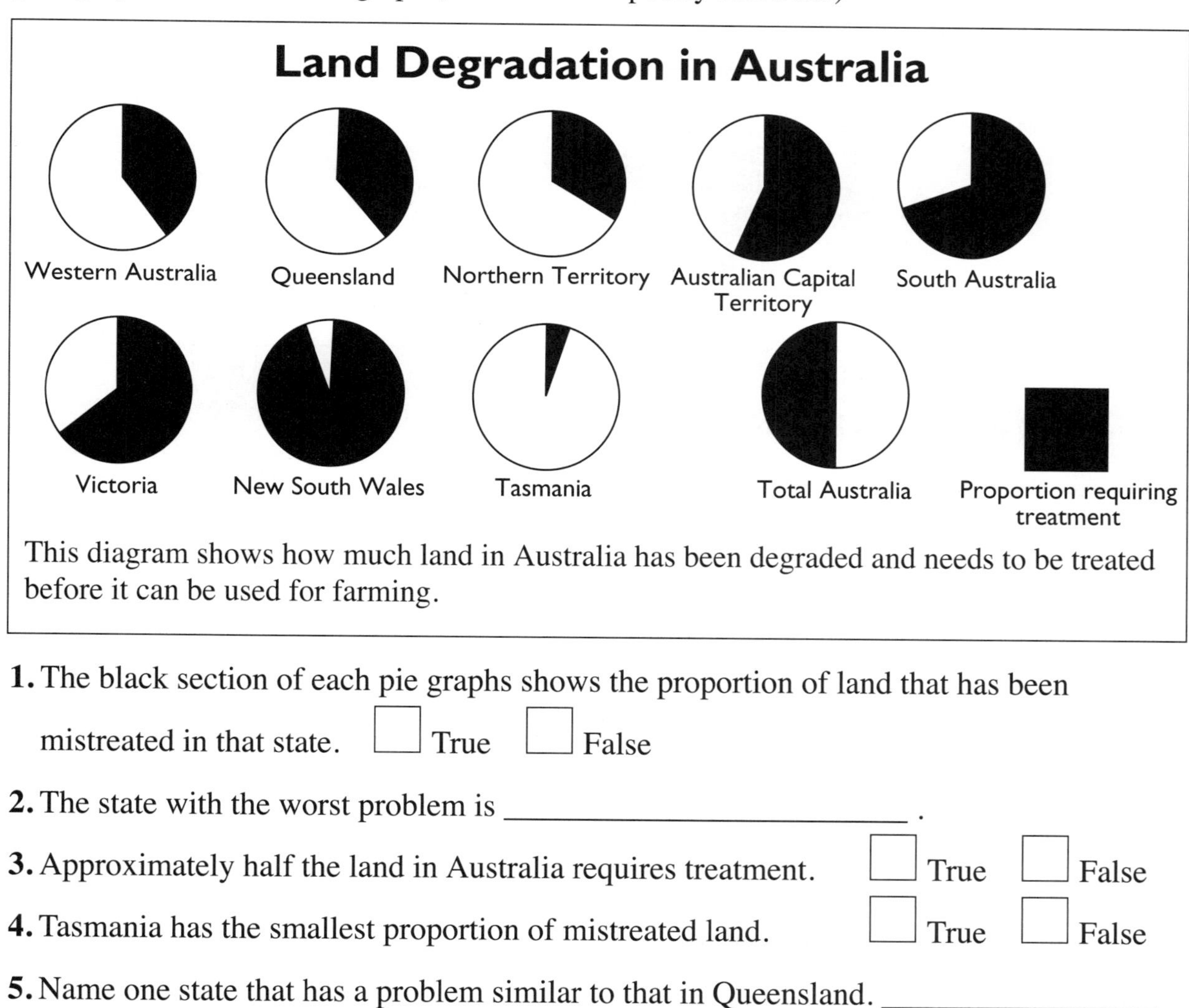

This diagram shows how much land in Australia has been degraded and needs to be treated before it can be used for farming.

1. The black section of each pie graphs shows the proportion of land that has been mistreated in that state. ☐ True ☐ False
2. The state with the worst problem is ________________________ .
3. Approximately half the land in Australia requires treatment. ☐ True ☐ False
4. Tasmania has the smallest proportion of mistreated land. ☐ True ☐ False
5. Name one state that has a problem similar to that in Queensland. ________________
6. The degraded land is no longer useful for ________________ .

Answers 1. True, 2. New South Wales, 3. True, 4. True, 5. Western Australia or Northern Territory, 6. farming

Understanding Graphs and Charts — Spacescape

The planet chart below comes from **Spacescape** by Karl Kruszelnicki (p. 10). It shows the planets and their moons.

The planets and their moons

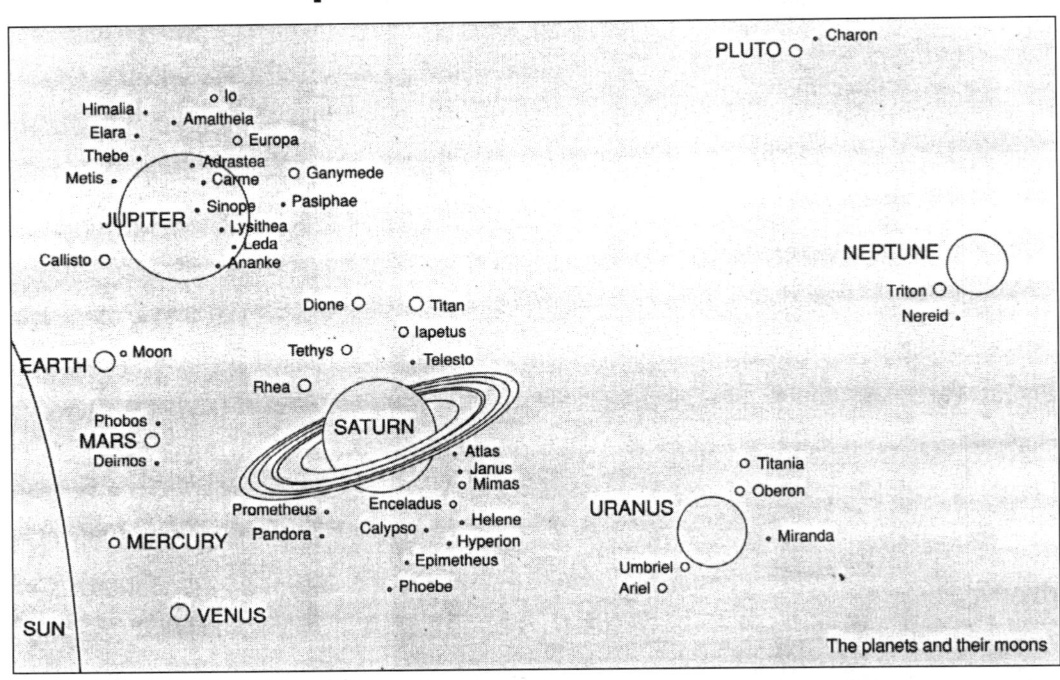

1. How many moons does Uranus have? ______________

2. The two planets without moons are ______________ and ______________.

3. Other than Earth, which other planet has only one moon? ______________

4. Draw a line from a planet to its moon.

Pluto	Phobos
Mars	Titan
Jupiter	Charon
Saturn	Oberon
Uranus	Ganymede

5. The planet closest to the sun is Mars. ☐ True ☐ False

6. Saturn's moon, Titan, is larger than the planet Mercury. ☐ True ☐ False

7. Write the numbers 1, 2, 3, and 4 in the boxes to show the planets according to the number of moons they have. (The planet with the least moons will be 1.)

☐ Neptune ☐ Earth ☐ Saturn ☐ Uranus